Management for Professionals

For further volumes:
http://www.springer.com/series/10101

Paul Vanderbroeck

Leadership Strategies for Women

Lessons from Four Queens on Leadership and Career Development

 Springer

Paul Vanderbroeck
Geneva
Switzerland

ISSN 2192-8096   ISSN 2192-810X (electronic)
ISBN 978-3-662-52475-6   ISBN 978-3-642-39623-6 (eBook)
DOI 10.1007/978-3-642-39623-6
Springer Heidelberg New York Dordrecht London

*For Joëlle, an accomplished woman
leader, and for Magdalena, that she
may become one.*

Preface

Almost 25 years ago, a few of my colleagues and I designed an "added value" system for people moves within Royal/Dutch Shell. For the company's population of managers and engineers throughout the world, we devised chains of moves: A replaces B replaces C, and so on. Our aim was to create value with every move, beyond merely filling a job. The added value might be in the form of a promotion, a developmental assignment, a coordinated move for a career couple, or an expatriation of a non-Brit or a Dutch employee. And, yes, sometimes it was a gender diversity move, although we did not use the word "diversity" back then. Even now, I do not see diversity as a goal in itself; adding value is the central aim. Integrating more women in the talent pool simply adds value to organizations and makes them perform better. From this perspective, I have worked at promoting gender diversity throughout my career as an HR executive and a leadership expert.

This book originates from my convictions that gender diversity is inherently advantageous for organizations and that the lessons of history are undervalued and underutilized in educational settings, especially management education. That doesn't mean leaders are constantly reinventing the wheel, but it does often lead them to make the same mistakes over and over again. As such, rather than offering a broad perspective, business schools have fallen victim to the same short-term thinking that has permeated organizations since the late twentieth century. Educating leaders to think in that way has, in my view, contributed to the worldwide financial and economic crisis that persists in 2013.

Many people have contributed to this book. First, I thank my wife Joëlle, who read every draft and, I might add, has successfully applied the book's lessons in her leadership practice. Second, I would like to acknowledge Professor Susan Schneider (HEC University of Geneva) for her unrelenting and challenging support. Finally, many thanks to two up-and-coming female leaders—Maaike Riesthuis and Geneviève van der Veen—for their diligent analysis and feedback. I am also indebted to the many female clients and fellow coaches who have consistently encouraged me to make this project happen.

Geneva, Switzerland
May 2013

Paul Vanderbroeck

Endorsements

"A wonderful selection of much-needed role models of powerful women who shaped their time with distinctively authentic styles, all their own. An inspiration for both men and women of what more gender balance in global political and economic roles has to offer the world."

Avivah Wittenberg-Cox, CEO 20-first and best-selling author of *Why Women Mean Business* and *How Women Mean Business.*

"We all know we can learn a lot from history. *Leadership Strategies for Women* does this in the unexpected context of gender diversity. Nicely written and original, the book is a powerful example of how looking back can help us moving forward."

Frank Uit de Weerd,
Vice-President HR Innovation, Research & Development, Royal Dutch/Shell

"An inspiring narrative that creatively leverages lessons from four women from the past, each of whom had to play the cards she was dealt, and each a force of nature who prevailed against the odds and shaped her world. Today's crop of aspiring women leaders, who often start from scratch and face a bewildering array of options and tough performance expectations, would do well to absorb this book's tightly drawn lessons."

Ingo Walter, Seymour Milstein Professor of Finance, Corporate Governance and Ethics, NYU Stern School of Business

Contents

Biography

Dr. Paul Vanderbroeck A historian by training and a former HR Executive, Dr. Paul Vanderbroeck is an international leadership expert who helps leaders in complex organizations to unleash their unique potential. Throughout his career, he has focused on the success of women leaders and the success of organizations by leveraging female talent. His research and experience as an executive coach have identified four obstacles to gender diversity and a set of methods to remove these. He works with corporations, nonprofit organizations, and business schools such as IMD and INSEAD. Paul is married to a woman who has her own successful leadership career as a senior civil servant. He is father of two children and currently lives in Geneva.

Introduction

How do women leaders make it to the top of an organization?
How can women stay at the top when most of their colleagues are men?
What should women do to exercise leadership well?

This book tells the stories of four powerful women who knew the answers to these three questions. Compelling as their stories are, recounting them is not enough to reveal why the women achieved so much. Therefore, this book also explicitly identifies the key factors in these leaders' career success, and it elucidates the competencies that enabled the women to exercise leadership effectively.

The four success stories offer women who already serve in leadership roles and those who aspire to become great leaders both inspiration and practical lessons that can be applied to real-world challenges. This book also provides advice to organizations that seek to improve the career success of their women leaders. Finally, it offers a fresh perspective for anyone interested in the topic of women leadership and careers.

1.1 Why This Book?

The topic of female leadership is frequently discussed in business schools, private corporations, public organizations, and political forums. Corollary subjects—to what extent women and men leaders differ, what it takes for women to have successful leadership careers, and why and how organizations should create a more gender-balanced leadership cadre—are widely covered in the management and self-help literature. An historical perspective on women's leadership, however, is not well represented. The treatises that do exist tend to approach the historical angle academically, in the vein of general interest ("tales of famous people"), or with an emphasis on recently elected political leaders.

Missing from the current offering is a comparative, long-range review of women leaders that examines their successes and failures to identify leadership competencies and deficiencies as lessons for modern women leaders. Given that a

P. Vanderbroeck, *Leadership Strategies for Women*, Management for Professionals,   1
DOI 10.1007/978-3-642-39623-6_1, © Springer-Verlag Berlin Heidelberg 2014

lack of role models is one of the factors that prevent women from reaching top positions in modern organizations, historical examples can fill the gap.

1.2   Why Women Leaders from History and Why These Four Queens?

The four case studies in this book—Cleopatra of Egypt, Isabella of Spain, Elizabeth I of England, and Catherine the Great of Russia—offer insights about leaders in free-market economies who shared our culture, thinking, and many of our values. Yet, because the economic and organizational systems of their eras were far less complex and changed much more slowly than ours, the connection between cause and effect is easier to discern. In that way, the study of history can help us better understand the implications of the choices and actions of contemporary and even future leaders. Thucydides, Ancient Greece's greatest historian, put it best: "An exact knowledge of the past [is] an aid to the interpretation of the future."[1]

Of course, our picture of the past is incomplete and, at least in part, subjective. Yet, let's face it, so is our picture of contemporary leaders, as made clear by the many, often contradictory arguments about how to approach gender diversity in leadership positions ("quota or no quota" to take just one example). Historical examples offer a unique alternative perspective: On the one hand, they are close enough to be recognizable; on the other, their distance in time permits us the luxury of learning from them without the contemporary political baggage and repercussions. It is difficult, for example, to admire Margaret Thatcher or Angela Merkel for their leadership qualities while simultaneously rejecting their politics. Whereas it should be possible to learn from Cleopatra without feeling compelled to endorse the killing of political rivals. Thus you can read in this book how Cleopatra lost her job because she acted like a man. And how she regained it by leveraging her difference as a woman.

In terms of career development—that is, rising to power and keeping it—queens have more in common with CEOs and leaders of nonprofit organizations than our modern political leaders do. The path to power of, for example, prime ministers in a democracy depends on success in elections, whereby the politician has to court voters at all levels of society. Queens and CEOs, in contrast, share the same tension between entitlement and competition. For queens, the entitlement follows from being part of a royal family. Actually reaching the throne and staying there, however, depends (among other things) on beating potential competitors who have a similar entitlement. For CEOs, the entitlement comes from being groomed or hired as a high-potential leader. Like queens, CEOs must beat competitors before

---

[1] Thucydides, *Peloponnesian War*, I.22 (Translation R. Crawley). Similarly Walsh, W. H. (1967). *Philosophy of history*. New York: Harper & Row, 196: *Our ultimate purpose in engaging in historical enquiries might not be just to find out the truth about what things were like in former times, but on the basis of that to make some comparison with the present.*

getting the top job—and then keep them at bay after assuming power. Unlike in elective politics, members at the lower levels of the organization have no say in who ascends to the top and becomes CEO. Catherine the Great, for example, followed a networking strategy that helped her to get to the top and stay there.

There are few examples of women in nonpolitical leadership roles prior to the twentieth century. Those who did act as leaders typically led family businesses, which make for poor comparisons with public companies and nonprofit organizations. Unlike women in ceremonial political leadership roles (e.g., Queen Victoria), formal political leaders hold real decision-making powers, have numerous opportunities to demonstrate general leadership traits, and make a significant impact on their environment. Assessing their leadership competencies is therefore easier, because there is more material to assess. As such these women leaders have more in common with the intended audience of this book.

Finally, I wanted to analyze winners, not losers, because I believe that winners offer the most useful lessons. The four queens represent the best of that very small class of women leaders. They reached the top of their organizations and can boast considerable achievements. In that vein, this book is about real women leaders who did both honorable and ignoble things with their talents to achieve greatness. They were not saints or heroes.

1.3   What Will You Find in This Book?

The first four chapters contain individual portraits of Cleopatra of Egypt (51–30 BC), Isabella of Spain (1451–1504), Elizabeth I of England (1533–1603), and Catherine the Great of Russia (1729–1796). These leadership biographies describe the life, career, and leadership behavior of each queen, with emphasis on the following questions:

- How did she reach her position of power?
- What critical career choices did she make—and with what consequences?
- What factors, individuals, and networks most influenced her career and behavior?
- How did she overcome adversity and competition?
- How did she combine work and family?
- What leadership challenges did she have to meet?
- What leadership competencies did she use to meet those challenges?
- Where was she successful—and where did she fail—as a leader? Why?
- What were her strengths and weaknesses?

The portraits also examine the period in which the leaders lived, to assess how well they met contemporary expectations of leadership. Near the end of each chapter is a discussion of the queen's overall impact as a leader, a cataloging of her strengths and weaknesses, and tips about what modern women can learn from this leader. The chapter closes with a list of the top five do's and don'ts that the queen's example offers as well as a bibliography that includes sources.

Each portrait gives special focus to one leadership competency or challenge that truly emblemized the leader. For example, Isabella's chapter is titled "A Woman with Visions." Twice Isabella displayed her ability to develop and realize a vision, which was the key to her success and place in history. Throughout her life, Isabella, who ruled the medieval kingdom of Castile in the fifteenth century, envisioned a united Spain under one crown. She realized this vision by joining with Ferdinand of Aragon, both in marriage and government, and by reconquering the lands of Spain still occupied by Moorish invaders. She also recognized Christopher Columbus's potential and sent him off on the mission that led him to the Americas.

Because the leaders are well known, the biographies offer enough information to remind readers of the key facts and context of each leader's life but do not concentrate on those elements. The focus, instead, is on the leader's path to power, leadership challenges and competencies, and comparisons among the four queens. A timeline summarizes the key stages and events of each queen's life.

Two chapters conclude the book. Chapter 6 compares the histories of the queens and articulates six overall lessons about how women can successfully develop their careers. This chapter also answers the question whether these women leaders actively promoted gender diversity. Chapter 7 first compares the four queens against the nine leadership competencies that their collective histories have yielded. These competencies are described in succinct, clear language that gives a nutshell overview of the queens' respective strengths and weaknesses. Next, nine leadership lessons for modern women are enumerated. Both chapters also contain advice for organizations on how to improve career management and leadership development for female staff.

1.4   How to Get the Most Out of This Book

In using this book, you may follow three different paths:
1. Read it the obvious way: from front to back, one queen at a time, followed by the two concluding chapters that offer practical lessons for you and your organization.
2. Read one of the four leadership portraits in Chaps. 2, 3, 4 and 5. Start with the queen who intrigues you most, or the one whose key challenge or competency (identified in the chapter title) you want to know more about. Then think about how the experience of this queen can inspire you and what practical lessons you can take from her example. The key do's and don'ts at the end of the chapter should be helpful in that regard. Later, you can read another chapter to find further inspiration and lessons.
3. Go straight to Chaps. 6 and 7 to glean the key lessons on career development and leadership. Each lesson contains short examples from the bios of the queens for illustration and explanation. If you want to know more, you can then consult the detailed leadership portraits in Chaps. 2, 3, 4 and 5.

1.5   **About the Research for This Book**

This book brings together my competencies as a historian, a leadership expert, and an executive coach for women. The fact that I am a historian (my published dissertation was on leadership in Ancient Rome) allowed me to access and interpret the historical data that we have at our disposal. I have drawn upon biographies and specific studies written by other scholars, as well as source material from the queens and their times. As an historian, I am aware that historical records are inherently incomplete and potentially biased. Therefore, I have accessed a breadth of sources: historical records, writings, speeches, archeological findings, visual expressions, and architecture.

As a leadership expert, I have made a leadership diagnosis of each of the four queens, in the way I normally do in my consulting and coaching practice. Through the historical data, I have assessed the behavior of the leaders in their professional contexts and, on that basis, have evaluated their leadership competencies. For example, Elizabeth I proved to be an excellent communicator, able to exploit a wide portfolio of instruments to influence her environment. In addition to competencies, I have also analyzed career progression to uncover key career-related success factors.

My expertise as an executive coach for women, my research on gender diversity, and my training as a historian together allow me to identify in the historical record the career and leadership competencies that are most relevant for women today. For example, I can offer historically informed but also practical advice about how women can make the most of their difference or minority status in the workplace.

Finally, the motivation for my research has been solely to find what really works for women leaders to make them successful in their careers and the exercise of leadership. This is also what drives me in my practice as a leadership expert. I am not interested in what "should be" in matters of gender equality or in what is politically acceptable. I'm interested in what gets practical results. This book will therefore offer few tips for favoring the women's cause from a political perspective. Yet the queens offer plenty of inspiration about how to make it in a man's world. Here is your opportunity to discover four fascinating female frontrunners.

Cleopatra VII of Egypt TIMETABLE (All dates are BC.)

69	Cleopatra born in Alexandria, Egypt
51	Succeeds her father as Queen of Egypt together with her younger brother Ptolemy XIII
49	Caesar crosses the Rubicon and starts a civil war against Pompey and the Roman Senate
48	Cleopatra thrown off the throne. Caesar arrives in Egypt
47	Death of Ptolemy XIII in battle with Caesar's army. Caesar reinstates Cleopatra as queen with her youngest brother Ptolemy XIV as co-ruler. Returns Cyprus to Egypt. Birth of Caesarion
46	Cleopatra's first visit to Rome
44	Second visit to Rome. Caesar assassinated. Roman civil war starts. Cleopatra has Ptolemy XIV killed and makes baby Caesarion co-ruler
42–41	Cleopatra's monetary reform
41	Roman civil war ends with a victory of the triumvirs Antony, Octavian, and Lepidus. Antony, the new Chairman of the JV with Egypt, and Cleopatra renew the JV alliance. At the behest of Cleopatra, Antony executes Arsinoe, a potential rival to the queen
40	Alexander and Cleopatra, twins, born to Antony and Cleopatra
36	Ptolemy born to Antony and Cleopatra
34	Donations of Alexandria: Cleopatra expands Egypt's territory thanks to Antony
33	Start of the civil war between Antony and Octavian
31	Antony and Cleopatra defeated at the Battle of Actium by Octavian
30	Cleopatra takes her own life at the age of 39

Cleopatra VII—credited with restoring Egypt back to the limelight in the face of the rising Roman Empire—is notorious for her conquests of powerful men, a life in luxury, and manipulative womanhood. However, when it comes to leadership, this young queen had more to offer than these one-sided presentations from romanticized fiction. She was an innovative change agent who pushed boundaries courageously, an effective influencer of stakeholders, and a master at developing and implementing strategies—just to mention a few of her impressive achievements. But before we explore precisely how Cleopatra executed her unique brand of leadership and why her example should matter to today's women leaders,

P. Vanderbroeck, *Leadership Strategies for Women*, Management for Professionals,
DOI 10.1007/978-3-642-39623-6_2, © Springer-Verlag Berlin Heidelberg 2014

Fig. 2.1 Bust of Cleopatra (Altes Museum, Berlin) (http://commons.wikimedia.org/wiki/File:Kleopatra-VII.-Altes-Museum-Berlin1.jpg)

let's first lay out some essential details about this fascinating leader's ascend to power (Fig. 2.1).

2.1   Life and Career

Cleopatra of Egypt was born in 69 BC, became queen at the age of 18, and ruled for 22 years from 51 to 30 BC, when she died by suicide in 30 BC at the age of 39. She was the last monarch of the Greek-Macedonian dynasty that reigned over Egypt for more than two centuries after Alexander the Great's conquest. She was therefore the descendant of Ptolemy I, one of Alexander's generals. She was well educated, spoke many languages, and became queen as part of a conventional succession plan: She inherited the throne after her father died. Although she had been prepared, it still should have taken her by surprise, because also in those days 18 were a young age to become queen of such a big country.

In Egypt at the time, women were prohibited by law from ruling independently. A female ruler was required to share the throne with—and defer power to—a man who was either her husband or her son. During the first 4 years of Cleopatra's reign, therefore, she led Egypt with one of her brothers, Ptolemy XIII, who was 8 years her junior. She did not do so submissively, however, and she relentlessly battled his advisers for power. After her brother's death at the age of 14, she was confirmed in her position by Julius Caesar. Henceforth she ruled with her youngest brother, Ptolemy XIV, this time easily taking the lead role, as various coins and papyri attest. Now secure in her position, Cleopatra was able to strengthen the joint venture (JV) alliance with Rome that her father, Ptolemy XII Auletes, had established, and she skillfully merged her professional goals with her personal life. Upon the birth of Caesarion, her son by Julius Caesar, Cleopatra instigated her brother's death and established the baby as her co-ruler. After Caesar's death, Cleopatra maintained the joint venture by forging an alliance with Caesar's former lieutenant, Marc Antony, with whom she had three children. This alliance allowed her to expand the territory und her command. During the final civil war, Antony and Cleopatra were defeated by Octavian's (the future emperor Augustus') fleet at Actium in 31 BC. Retreating to Egypt, Cleopatra had a number of potential adversaries killed and pocketed their money to increase her own bargaining power. Antony having committed suicide and Cleopatra's negotiations with Octavian failing to provide a result, she made an end to her life and her reign in 30 BC at the age of 39.

2.2   Key Leadership Challenges

When Cleopatra became queen she took on the following challenges:
- Directing her career;
- Managing Egypt's joint venture with Rome;
- Moving her country from loss to profit; and
- Ensuring her own succession

2.2.1   The Path to Power and Career Management

For 100 years before Cleopatra took the helm, the ruling house of Egypt was ridden with tension and conflict, and the country suffered from a lack of direction. When Cleopatra and young Ptolemy XIII took the throne, the "managers" (the court) of Egypt's "headquarters" (the capital city of Alexandria) resented being ruled by a woman and strife continued. Cleopatra compensated first by acting as a man. The images that portray Cleopatra show her wearing male garb; perhaps she hoped to appear more like a "female king" than a queen. And it's possible that she tried to suppress her femininity in her behavior as well—at least before she met Caesar. Second, she emphasized her identification with Egypt. Rather than confine her efforts to Hellenistic Alexandria, she sought support throughout the country.

Though Cleopatra initially gained the upper hand—coins and other images show that she positioned herself as more important than her brother—she ultimately lost that advantage, possibly during a time of drought that may have undermined her position and credibility. When Ptolemy XIII's advisers finally took power and got Rome to recognize his authority, Cleopatra retreated and recruited an army to start a civil war. When Julius Caesar landed in Egypt and seized power, he summoned Cleopatra and Ptolemy to Alexandria to end the dispute. He said that he wanted to reestablish the status quo ante, as per the testament of their father, with both siblings on the throne.

This is when Cleopatra started her love affair with Caesar, her JV counterpart. Whereas Cleopatra never married Caesar, it should be noted that in antiquity it was quite common to forge political alliances through marriage and parenthood. Let us look at Cleopatra's situation from a modern leadership perspective: She had only recently acquired the throne, and her authority was already undermined by internal competition. At the same time, Caesar, who was not only more powerful than Cleopatra but also her greatest competitor for Egypt, began to hunger for a takeover. She decided that the wisest course of action would be to negotiate the best possible deal for her own career and for the organization she was leading. Her brother's advisers, however, remained hostile to Caesar and attacked the Roman army. Caesar gained the upper hand and Ptolemy XIII lost his life. Cleopatra was reinstalled on the throne, now with her youngest brother Ptolemy XIV.

Yet Cleopatra still faced the problem of legitimacy in terms of her right to rule independently. She used motherhood in several ways to validate her position as queen, as will be discussed later. She gave birth to children with a legitimate claim to the throne. She also battled the problem by removing competitors who were a threat to her primacy. Over time, she schemed against one brother and did away with another brother and a sister through assassination. Yet, while her siblings did indeed pose a serious threat to Cleopatra, and although there was much precedent in Egypt's ruling family, murder was nevertheless considered to be unacceptable. So here we meet Cleopatra's dark side. She certainly is a powerful deviation from the (inaccurate) perception that women leaders are less inclined to break rules (as if Lehman "Sisters" would not have gone bust).

As queen, she had plenty of help in combining work and motherhood. Most of the time, the fathers of her children were away managing their own careers. It is intriguing that the gaps in the written records of Cleopatra's reign coincide with the latter part of her pregnancies and the first few years after each birth. Possibly, Cleopatra took a time-out to ensure the success of each pregnancy and to nurture her newborn children. During those times she delegated the ruling of the kingdom to the royal administration, now rid of the misogynistic senior civil servants that had caused her trouble in the beginning of her reign.

2.2.2 Managing the Joint Venture with Rome

Cleopatra's father had depended on Rome, the mightiest power in the Mediterranean world, to maintain his hold on the throne. For that reason, and perhaps also because he was worried about leaving Egypt in the hands of two young siblings, his testament stipulated that Rome should henceforward act as the protector of his dynasty. In modern terms this translates into Rome having just taken an important stake in its JV partner and one or two important seats on the board, including the position of chairman, when Cleopatra and her brother inherited the throne.

Rich in corn, ships, and manpower, Egypt served as a critical supply base for Rome. By that time the demand for food in the bustling city of Rome and the center of power far outstripped the supplies of Italy. For Caesar, Cleopatra's offer of an alliance, as opposed to an acquisition was attractive: He could have access to Egypt's resources without giving a strong power base to a Roman governor and potential competitor. For her part, Cleopatra could secure the independence of the realm, shore up her own power-base, and regain Cyprus. Though Cleopatra was a fairly inexperienced high potential (with a less-than-perfect track record), Caesar saw her aptitude and was willing to give her a chance. As per her father's testament, Caesar had the authority to appoint Egypt's ruler. After recognizing Cleopatra's authority to represent the important JV partner, he leveraged his position as the chairman of the JV to put some checks and balances in place. He left four legions in Egypt tasked with propping up Cleopatra's power base and, if she should fall out of power, assuring Rome's control.

Cleopatra visited headquarters in Rome for the first time in 46 BC, together with her young co-ruler, Ptolemy XIV. During this trip and through her alliance with Caesar, she managed to reestablish Egypt as a friend and ally of the Roman people, just as her father had done. With this recognition, she confirmed the country's status as JV partner and forestalled any takeover plans. Apparently by now she had successfully proved herself in the eyes of the chairman to merit such recognition.

In 44 BC, during one of Cleopatra's trips to Rome for strategic discussions about the future of Egypt, Caesar was assassinated. Afterward, it seems Cleopatra was unsure how to proceed. She kept a low profile while the conflict between Caesar's assassins and his heirs played out. When the rival parties agreed that Caesar's political acts would remain in force, the move guaranteed that the joint venture with Rome, Caesar's appointment of Cleopatra, and the return of Cyprus to Egypt would not be revoked.

During Rome's civil war of 44–41 BC, Cleopatra was courted by different parties to provide resources, but she did not choose sides. The triumvirs Octavian, Lepidus, and Marc Antony eventually won the war, with Antony taking over the chairmanship of the JV with Egypt, since he now ruled the eastern part of the Roman empire. In 41 BC, 3 years after Caesar's death and the end of the war, Antony summoned Cleopatra to Asia Minor for an explanation of her behavior during the civil war.

The discussion turned out to be a challenging performance appraisal. But even though Cleopatra was only 28 years old, she had ruled Egypt for 10 years, and thus she handled the interview well. In addition to assertively arguing her cause and offering proof of how she had responded to calls from Antony's allies, she took advantage of the opportunity to seduce him and make him her ally. The alliance became so strong that Antony arranged for the murder of Cleopatra's last remaining claimant and rival to the throne of Egypt: her sister Arsinoe. The children born to Antony and Cleopatra further strengthened this alliance.

Because Antony needed Cleopatra to fund his military campaigns, her position in the JV grew more important. He gave her control over large territories that in the past had belonged to the empire of her ancestors.

When Antony and another of Caesar's heirs, Octavian, fell out with each other in 33 BC, another civil war erupted. Cleopatra continued to support Antony, and when he lost decisively at Actium, she tried to negotiate the best possible deal that she could. She offered to resign in exchange for her treasure, and she tried to pass power to her children, hoping to leave them the legacy of an independent Egypt. She was unsuccessful in both efforts, however, and the story ends with Cleopatra's suicide and the annexation of Egypt by Rome.

In the aftermath, however, Cleopatra's youngest children were well treated, and Egypt retained its special status in the Roman Empire. Directly governed by the Emperor, it was allowed to prosper and hold on to its position as a key provider of resources, which was a distinct improvement over the traditional lot of conquered territories (Fig. 2.2).

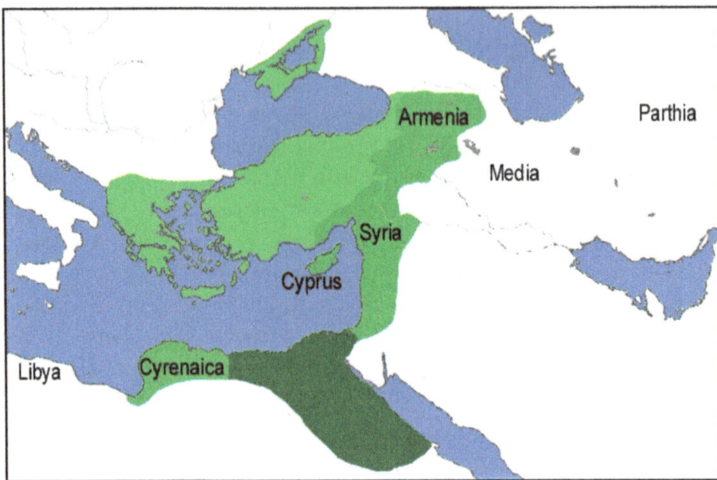

Fig. 2.2 Map showing Egypt and the four territories Cleopatra received from the Romans: Cyprus, Cyrenaica, Syria, and Armenia (http://commons.wikimedia.org/wiki/File:Donations_of_ Alexandria_34BC.gif)

2.2.3 From Loss to Profit

When Cleopatra rose to the throne, Egypt was in dire straits both economically and politically. The nation had lost several territories (Cyprus, Cyrenaica, and Syria) to the Romans and suffered famines as a result of disappointing harvests and Nile flooding. What's more, Egypt still owed a big debt to Rome. Cleopatra seemed to manage these challenges reasonably well, since there were no uprisings or other signs of trouble. And there is evidence that in 42–41 BC, when the Nile did *not* flood, she effectively fought the resulting inflation by issuing coins with a reduced bronze weight but an unchanged nominal value—a first in antiquity. Cleopatra also took measures to alleviate the tax burden and provide the capital with sufficient food.

Cleopatra developed a vision for Egypt during the first part of her reign: to avoid being conquered and to stay independent of Rome. Yet she knew that Egypt could not survive on its own, given the current state of affairs. She shared this vision with her organization to inspire and motivate her people, at least implicitly: She was the first of her dynasty to learn Egyptian, she actively involved herself in Egyptian religious life, and she generously provided funds to temples and cults. (Thanks to this she could muster an army once her husband-brother and his surroundings had ousted her from power just before Caesar's arrival.) The strategy she developed allowed Egypt to grow stronger and become more profitable. And thanks to her personal relationships with Caesar and then Antony, the JV became a cooperative partnership as opposed to the first stage of a take-over.

During the last 10 years of Cleopatra's reign, Egypt experienced a period of economic growth. Once again having forged strong partnership with a top Roman leader, the queen felt she had secured her first vision of preventing a takeover. She began to focus on a second, bolder goal: to reinstate the Ptolemaic empire, which once reached well beyond Egypt, to its old splendor. It probably also included an end to the JV, either by going separate ways or by a full merger with the eastern part of the Roman Empire. It is not quite clear whether Cleopatra or Antony developed this new vision (it may have been a compromise between the two), but both certainly shared and expressed it. Ultimately, however, Antony's ambition may have been even more expansive than Cleopatra's: He seems to have set his sights on recreating the empire of Alexander the Great.

This time around, Cleopatra used the vision to motivate and inspire her people. Coins were issued with joint portraits of Antony and Cleopatra, and she chose their children's names—Alexander Helios, Cleopatra Selene, and Ptolemy Philaldelphos—with care. In 34 BC, Antony gave Cleopatra and their three children command over additional territories in a very public ceremony. During the event, known as the Donations of Alexandria, Alexander was dressed as a king of Media, formerly a part of Persia and Alexander the Great's greatest conquest. Ptolemy Philaldelphos (named after his ancestor Ptolemy II, who ruled over the empire at its prime) was dressed as a Macedonian, the country from which Alexander and the Ptolemies originated. At the end of the ceremony, Cleopatra declared the commencement of a new era.

The strategy for realizing this vision hinged on Egypt becoming an important supplier of corn, ships, money, and manpower to Rome. In return, Rome granted Cleopatra control of Cyprus, Crete, Libya, and part of Syria.

The vision was never realized, however, and one can only speculate as to why. Perhaps Cleopatra underestimated the strength of Rome and its reluctance to share power. Or perhaps Egypt simply succumbed to the vicissitudes of war, as Antony could well have won at Actium.

2.3   Key Leadership Competencies

2.3.1   Vision and Strategy Development

Cleopatra's first vision—of independence from Rome—was not unrealistic. It must have been inspirational to many of those around her, particularly the top managers in the Ptolemean administration, whose positions would be first on the line in case of a Roman takeover. The inhabitants of Hellenistic Alexandria also probably took heart in her efforts, since they had never welcomed Caesar and had risen in revolt against him. They had a fierce desire for independence and realized that economically they would be better off as an independent center of trade and industry. And the rest of Egypt may have warmed up to the idea of protection implied in the vision and emphasized by Cleopatra, who intentionally portrayed herself as Egypt's queen mother.

Yet her second, much bolder vision, of growth and market share, was even more compelling. National pride in regaining strength once again—along with the consequent revenue, tax, and business opportunities—was motivating. This is why Cleopatra misrepresented her return from Actium after Antony's defeat as a victory to the people at home. The truth would have caused her to lose all support.

Cleopatra's goal was for Egypt to become critically important, even indispensable, to Rome and to prove more valuable as a JV partner than as an acquisition. The strategy she developed to realize her visions both accounted for Egypt's market position as a significant player in the Mediterranean (though far less powerful than Rome) and made the most of Egypt's key assets—corn, manpower, and ships. As a supply base, Egypt had no equal, and Rome was hungry for resources, particularly in times of civil war. Shrewdly, Cleopatra was able to get additional territories in return for responding to that demand, and Alexandria—the Rotterdam of antiquity—greatly benefited from its role as the trade capital of the Mediterranean. Cleopatra developed two related inspirational visions and a workable strategy for both, i.e. growth through becoming Rome's key supplier of critical resources, which she implemented successfully.

2.3.2   Generating Positive Change

Cleopatra successfully pushed against the boundaries of her reign and generated positive change for both herself and her organization. Though she was forced to reign with a co-ruler, she learned how to effectively put herself forward as the dominant leader and thus overcome the gender bias against her: Ruling on behalf of her infant son, she was no longer required to be *married* to a male co-ruler.

She also elevated Egypt's position in the joint venture with Rome. Egypt clearly was the junior partner during Caesar's reign, but Cleopatra equalized the relationship during her alliance with Marc Antony.

Like all leaders, from kings and queens to CEOs, Cleopatra knew she had to establish a successor, which in her case meant producing at least one heir. In Egypt for centuries, the children of the royal family were the result of marriages between kin. Yet here, too, she pushed boundaries. Rather than producing offspring with one of her brothers, as might have been expected, she chose Caesar and Antony—who came from outside her family and held powerful positions in Rome—to father her children. She purposefully developed successors who could bridge the gap between the two partners in the joint venture.

2.3.3   Leveraging Difference

When she first became the head of her organization, Cleopatra fell into the same trap as some of her predecessor queens in Egypt had done and as many female corporate executives do today: She emulated male behavior (Fig. 2.3). For this reason, Cleopatra was not particularly popular in the beginning of her reign, and Ptolemy XIII's sycophants were able to get rid of her.

Fig. 2.3 Relief showing Cleopatra (on the *right*, dressed as a male pharao) and Isis (Musée du Louvre, Paris) (http://commons.wikimedia.org/wiki/File:Cleopatra_Isis_Louvre_E27113.jpg)

Cleopatra learned from that experience and fully leveraged her femininity when she met Caesar. In modern terms, Cleopatra essentially slept with her boss. But in the first century BC, political alliances were also formed through marriages and parenthood, so it would be wrong to apply a modern filter to their relationship.

Much has been written about the first time Cleopatra and Caesar met, when she is said to have surprised him by rolling out of a bundled carpet. Most historians today see the event as a clever, deliberate, and successful attempt by Cleopatra to seduce Caesar, though some believe it was the more mature Caesar who took advantage of the opportunity. Or maybe Cleopatra hid in the carpet only to escape detection by her brother's guards, who controlled access to Caesar, and not to impress the Roman general. In any case, most agree that Cleopatra was enchanting (if not necessarily beautiful).

The historian Dio Cassius, otherwise a sensationalist, in this case gives us a clue of what, may have really happened. Cleopatra had been granted an audience with Caesar: In his roles as Chairman of the JV and guardian of Ptolemy Auletes' will, Caesar's original plan was simply to reinstate both siblings on the throne. Anticipating the meeting, Cleopatra then *adorned and beautified herself so as to appear before him in the most majestic and at the same time pity-inspiring guise.*[1]

---

[1] Dio Cassius, *Roman History,* 42.34.6 (translation Loeb).

In other words, she dressed smartly for the occasion, just like any modern executive on the first meeting with his or her new boss. So far so good. But what made the difference was that Cleopatra effectively used a positive female archetype to get Caesar's attention: the "damsel in distress" or "Helen of Troy"—a noble maiden in need of the hero's support. An archetype is an image locked in our collective unconscious that reflects key roles in our society as they are defined through literature, art, and mythology—the "original". Cleopatra could have attempted to force her way through her brother's blockade—she had an army outside the gates—but she chose to go to Caesar humbly instead, asking for help. And he probably melted in front of this vulnerable creature. The rest is history.

Cleopatra, however, was careful not to let this archetype turn into a stereotype, which is a simplified image of a particular type of person and based on exaggerated characteristics and therefore usually a caricature—the "knockoff". After defeating her elder brother and reinstalling Cleopatra on the throne with her second brother, Caesar embarked on a Nile cruise with her. Though the trip was no doubt pleasant and perhaps romantic for them, it also left no doubt among the Egyptians that Cleopatra was their queen—in charge and not a mere dependent of Caesar's. She later reconfirmed this image in Rome, during her first trip there in 46 BC.

The idea of the "road show on the Nile" to publicly display Cleopatra's authority was the result of Caesar's mentoring of this young high potential queen. Behind Caesar's successful career stood—among other things—his excellent and innovative reputation management. For example he invented embedded journalism. During his conquest of Gaul, he had his military exploits read out to the public back in Rome. Caesar was acutely aware of Cleopatra's reputational risks. He was concerned that Egyptians and Romans alike might balk at a woman ruler. Therefore not only did he nominate her head of Egypt, but he actually set her up for success, something many modern CEO's and chairmen still fail to do. Caesar propped up her power base with a few legions and it was his suggestion that Cleopatra should marry her youngest brother. That way, at least nominally she would be conforming to the tradition of women not ruling alone. Before Caesar, Cleopatra's acting like a man had cost her the throne. She got it back by leveraging her femininity. It should be no surprise that Cleopatra's visual representations of herself after meeting Caesar show her no longer as a male Pharao but in female dress (Fig. 2.4).

Upon her return from Rome and after the birth of her son, Cleopatra started to exploit a second positive archetype to leverage her difference: the mother. When Cleopatra got rid of her co-ruler brother and installed Caesarion in his place, she cultivated an image of herself as the mythological goddess Isis, a single mother like Cleopatra, who had ruled as queen consort until her baby Horus became adult. On coins from her early reign, before she was kicked out, Cleopatra appears alone and with stern features. When she got back on the throne, coins were minted showing her holding baby Caesarion. Cleopatra clearly wanted to highlight the fact that she was the queen mother of the future king of Egypt. But even further, she wanted to be seen as the mother of all Egyptians. And since she actually spoke their language, which was rather uncommon for the members of her dynasty, and actively participated in the religion of the local population, the idea was not too far-fetched.

Fig. 2.4 Relief showing Cleopatra (now on the *left*, dressed as a woman) and Caesarion (Temple of Denderah, Egypt) (http://commons.wikimedia. org/wiki/File:Denderah3_Cleopatra_Cesarion. jpg)

After Caesar's death and the ensuing civil war, Cleopatra effectively used a third positive archetype: the seductress. Dressed up as Venus with the full imagery and symbolism of Greco-Roman mythology, she overcame any initial doubts that Marc Antony may have had of her intentions. The move proved to be an effective door opener for negotiations with him to revise the joint venture, which became even more advantageous for Egypt than it had been under Caesar. In her discussions with Antony, Cleopatra showed her strength at building rapport, matching both his humor and his penchant for parties. Again, Cleopatra was careful not to let the archetype turn into a stereotype, and soon she was once more queen and mother to her people.

Cleopatra most certainly knew how to get the attention of two powerful men. From a modern perspective, one could say that Cleopatra displayed an effective use of her difference in the workplace. Because of her gender, she was able to open doors in ways that others were not. And by evoking positive female archetypes, she stood out from the legions of standard male executives (generals or foreign monarchs). Those skills and attributes certainly made her interesting and perhaps even less threatening: Certainly a man would not have survived surprising Rome's greatest soldier in a carpet.

2.3.4   Building and Maintaining a Network

Cleopatra had the opportunity to observe how her father handled his relationships with stakeholders in Rome. Ptolemy Auletes severely indebted his country when he secured Rome's protection with cash (the equivalent of almost half Egypt's annual GDP). He tried to recover the funds by hiring a Roman expatriate as CFO, but the effort was unsuccessful. The burden of repayment then fell to Cleopatra, who may well have vowed not to become too dependent on the Romans after that experience.

Cleopatra visited headquarters in Rome twice while with Caesar. In addition to reinforcing her legitimacy as the queen of Egypt and preventing a takeover by Rome, she exploited her difference so as to get a lot of attention and publicity. As a woman leader, smartly and very differently dressed, she stood out and was the talk of the town. However, she failed to leverage this attention, which would make it very easy to get in touch with people, into an effective network. For example, she snubbed Cicero by failing to deliver on her promise to get him a rare book from the library in Alexandria. Cicero may not have had much power, but as an opinion leader and prolific writer and speaker he had tremendous influence.

Cleopatra's intercultural networking was below par as well. She failed to see that although Rome was well under way to becoming a monarchy, republican values were still held in high regard. She might have had better success if she realized that influence did not depend on being close only to the top leader. Similarly, Rome had not yet become a multinational concern. Though several nations were involved in the organization, it was run from Roman headquarters with expatriate managers, and thus Roman culture prevailed. Therefore, since networking was important in Rome, it should have been important to Cleopatra as well. But to her, building relationships with more than one player might have seemed more like intrigue than networking. She also did not realize that the ostentatious display of wealth by a woman was an impression that needed managing.

Cleopatra communicated only indirectly (that is, mainly through her court retinue) with Romans she would have considered of lower rank. She must have gained a lot of intelligence from those encounters, but when processed through the filter of eastern monarchy, she may have interpreted them incorrectly. As a semi democratic city-state, Rome was much more informal and egalitarian than Egypt, and Cleopatra was not used to its customs. Dignitaries, politicians, and women of high station mingled in the streets with commoners going about their business. Roman women were quite influential behind the scenes, both economically and politically, but they were not allowed to hold formal leadership positions. As a female executive in Rome, therefore, Cleopatra was an anomaly.

Though she was a guest in Caesar's house, Cleopatra was the subject of gossip and scorn. Yet Romans probably cared less about Cleopatra's status as the mistress of a man married to a Roman matron than they did about her possible influence on Caesar's increasingly regal behavior. Others' suspicion that Caesar wanted to become king, after all, was what got him killed.

It seems that Cleopatra was oblivious to all that. Once he died in 44 BC, she may have expected that someone else would simply take over. So she was at a loss when that did not happen and civil war broke out. She found herself without a network to proactively influence her situation and provide her with a better view of the issues at play. Committing the plentiful resources of Egypt to the war could well have tipped the balance in favor of one of the parties, who would have been very grateful to her. Instead, she waited things out, holding off on requests to meet and provide resources. She got a break when Antony summoned her and she could once more

Fig. 2.5 Bust of Marc Antony (Vatican Museums, Rome; © akg-images)

leverage her difference as a woman by incarnating Venus to favor her position. She managed to convince him of her importance as a partner (Fig. 2.5).

Still, she did not learn. Once allied with Antony, she focused on him exclusively and spurned influential Romans in his entourage, many of whom changed sides to Octavian. She behaved similarly with Rome's other JV partners, such as Herod, the king of Judea. Antony had given Judea to Herod to rule, but he reserved some key areas of revenue (bitumen and balsam) for Cleopatra. The recipients were charged with negotiating the details, and Cleopatra went for and obtained a win-lose deal. Not the best way to construct a fruitful peer relationship.

There are indications that Herod actively tarnished Cleopatra's reputation by reinforcing the negative stereotype of the seductress and sexual predator. Herod, although much less important to the Romans, was an excellent networker. Though he was initially allied with Antony and Cleopatra, he managed to survive the civil war unscathed, and his position was confirmed by Octavian. Herod then lived long enough to make life difficult for Jesus Christ and His parents.

It is worth looking at Cleopatra's behavior around the decisive battle of Actium in 31 BC. The Roman historian Plutarch describes how Cleopatra convinced Antony to accept her presence against the advice of his generals. She argued that not only did she bring more resources to the battle but also that she had successfully governed a kingdom that was larger than the realms of any of the other allied kings present, even though she was a woman. Just like when she first met Antony, she based her arguments on facts and they were certainly valid. However, Cleopatra was unaware of how others saw her and thus neglected to take that significant factor into account. She nor any of the other rulers would be considered a match to an experienced Roman general on the battlefield. But even more, while female leaders were not unheard of in Egypt and some other nations, the concept of women in official leadership positions was completely alien to the Romans. Stay-at-home, dutiful matrons were venerated in Rome, a stereotype embodied by Octavia, Antony's official wife and his adversary's sister. Cleopatra' blind spot was not realizing that being Antony's mistress *and* a "career woman" disqualified her in the eyes of the average Roman. Hence, Antony's generals were right to point out that her presence gave Antony's adversaries a lot of ammunition for propaganda.[2]

After Antony's defeat, Cleopatra stood alone against her Roman enemies. Because of insufficient networking she failed to manage her reputation effectively. One of the archetypes she used so successfully, the seductress, turned into a stereotype and gave her bad press in Rome, which was exploited by both Caesar's and Antony's enemies. There was no one to plead her cause in the final dealings with Octavian. Rather the contrary: Some of the people she had rubbed the wrong way at Actium showed up in Octavian's entourage when he came to claim his victory. Cleopatra, it would seem, had not benefited enough from Julius Caesar's mentoring in reputation management.

Cleopatra's example shows that linguistic ability without empathy or intercultural intelligence can actually be a disadvantage in building and maintaining a network. She was known for the fact that she spoke many languages. With educated Romans, she conversed in Greek. She would have been able to speak with Herod in his own language. Being fluent in a language, however, clearly does not guarantee an understanding of thoughts, feelings, and values.

Cleopatra built effective professional and personal relationships with both Caesar and Antony, and those relationships did not infringe on any ethical limits of her organization or its local social environment. They helped her rule for more than two decades, achieve growth through acquisitions, and leave Egypt protected by a special status within the Roman Empire.

On the other hand, building intense personal relationships with a small number of individuals prevented Cleopatra from developing strong ties with other key players. And because her fortunes were so strongly linked with Antony's, Cleopatra was dragged down with him when civil war broke out again. Keeping a greater distance from Antony and forming a closer relationship with Octavian and his entourage might have allowed her to preserve Egypt's independence longer.

2.4   Cleopatra's Leadership Impact

By strengthening the joint venture between Egypt and Rome, Cleopatra saved her country from a hostile Roman takeover that would have resulted in a loss of autonomy, fatalities, and grave economic consequences. Furthermore, it was because of Cleopatra that Egypt was awarded the special status of an imperial province, with accompanying benefits, when the nation did eventually succumb. And the relationship proved to be truly a joint venture in that best practices were exchanged. Caesar, for example, used Egyptian astronomers to establish the Julian calendar of 365 days, which remained in effect in the Western world until 1582, when it was replaced by the Gregorian calendar.

---

[2] Actually, Octavian used the fact that Antony had delegated authority to a woman as the *casus belli* and declared war on Cleopatra, not Antony: Plutarch, *Antony,* 60.

2.5   What Women Can Learn from This Leader

Based on the discussion above, we come to the following performance appraisal

Leadership Challenge	Rating
Career Direction	*Partly Achieved*
Managing the Joint Venture	*Fully Achieved*
Regain Profitability	*Fully Achieved*
Succession Management	*Partly Achieved*

and leadership assessment of Cleopatra.

Leadership Competency	Rating
Vision and Strategy Development	*Competent*
Generating Positive Change	*Strong*
Leveraging Difference	*Strong*
Building and Maintaining a Network	*Needs Development*

Cleopatra used an effective combination of leadership competencies to realize her achievements. In addition, she smartly overcame the discrimination against her sex that did not allow her to dominate the throne. Nevertheless, as the series of premeditated murders she instigated attest, she also had a dark side and was a ruthless and cunning leader.

Cleopatra was born into a society in which women enjoyed greater rights and liberties than did their counterparts in other contemporary societies such as Rome. And they were even allowed to run the country, albeit in partnership with, or on behalf of, men. This, and the excellent education she had received in her youth, certainly put her in a good starting position for her career. Yet even in Egypt she met resistance as a woman leader from senior managers in the administration. She was apparently oblivious to the attitude towards gender in Rome, her senior JV partner. Thus at home and towards headquarters in Rome she consciously and unconsciously had to fight, not always successfully, against being relegated to second best. We can only speculate what this meant for her psychologically.

Perhaps she was fooled by the recognition she received from Julius Caesar and Marc Antony. We have no indication that Cleopatra did anything to mitigate the misunderstanding and outright hostility she met as a woman leader from the Romans. For instance, she could have tried to exploit the mother archetype to convey a positive, acceptable image of a woman leader in Roman culture—especially since the son she had with Caesar accompanied her during her trips to Rome. It is intriguing that she was not able to make this cultural leap, particularly when taking into consideration that she already had effectively used the mother-hood archetype in a similar situation in Egypt: When meeting resistance as a woman during her first years as a queen, she first tried to put up a masculine face. That cost her the throne. When she got her position back, she used the motherhood archetype, which did work.

Cleopatra developed a vision and a strategy that were ambitious, inspiring, and in line with the realities of her organization and its context. Later, perhaps because she became overconfident or was unable to bring Antony down to reality, she developed an unrealistic and unsustainable new vision.

Cleopatra demonstrated the power of extending relationships beyond the professional and into the personal. At the same time she incurred great risks by allying herself with only one individual at a time. Her greatest flaw was her inability to build and maintain an effective network, particularly across borders. Consequently, she became supremely vulnerable when her partner was taken out of the picture. Not knowing whom to influence put her in a passive position, unable to proactively influence the power plays. Failing a network, she lacked understanding about the organizational culture of the Romans to effectively manage her reputation.

Cleopatra's strongest feature was her ability to turn her difference into an opportunity. She used positive archetypes, unique to women and difficult to exploit by a man, effectively. She can be an inspiration to women leaders in how to be successful by distinguishing themselves from, rather than imitating, male behavior.

2.6   Top Five Do's and Don'ts from Cleopatra

- Do
  - Come back after a failure
  - Get close to your workforce
  - Develop strong relationships with powerful stakeholders
  - Be innovative in generating change
  - Turn your difference as a woman into an opportunity
- Don't
  - Forget to network to protect your reputation
  - Act like man; it may cost you your job
  - Follow your boss' strategy under all circumstances
  - Underestimate the importance of cultural differences
  - Focus not only on the "what" but also on the "how" of your message

Bibliography

Appian, *The civil wars* (in Greek).

Caesar, J. *The Alexandrian wars* (in Latin).

Cassius Dio, *Roman history* (in Greek).

Cicero, M. T., *Letters to Atticus* (in Latin).

Gruen, E. (2003). Cleopatra in Rome: Facts and fantasies. In D. Braund & C. Gill (Eds.), *Myth, history, and culture in Republican Rome* (pp. 257–274). Exeter: University of Exeter Press.

Plutarch, *Lives of Antony, Caesar, Pompey* (in Greek).

Pomeroy, S. B. (1975). *Goddesses, whores, wives, and slaves: Women in classical antiquity.* New York: Schocken.

Riad, S. (2011). Invoking Cleopatra to examine the shifting ground of leadership. *The Leadership Quarterly, 22,* 831–850.

Roller, D. W. (2010). *Cleopatra: A biography.* Oxford: Oxford University Press.

Schiff, S. (2010). *Cleopatra: A life.* New York: Little, Brown and Company.

Suetonius Tranquillus, G. *Julius Caesar, Augustus* (in Latin).

Thompson, D. J. (1994). Egypt, 146–31 B.C. In J. A. Crook, A. Lintott, & E. Rawson (Eds.), *The Cambridge ancient history. Second Edition. Volume IX: The last age of the Roman Republic, 146–43 B.C* (pp. 310–326). Cambridge: Cambridge University Press.

Tyldesley, J. (2008). *Cleopatra: Last queen of Egypt.* New York: Basic Books.

Vanderbroeck, P. (2010). The traps that keep women from reaching the top and how to avoid them. *The Journal of Management Development, 29* (9), 764–770.

Isabella of Spain TIMETABLE

1451	Isabella born in Castile, on of the Kingdoms on the Iberian Peninsula
1461	Isabella moves to live at the court of her half-brother, Enrique IV, King of Castile
1468	Isabella becomes crown princess of Castile
1469	Marries Ferdinand of Aragon
1474	Enrique dies. Isabella claims the throne of Castile. Start of the civil war
1475	Isabella shares power in Castile with Ferdinand
1476	Isabella and Ferdinand put a victorious end to the civil war
1479	Ferdinand becomes King of Aragon
1480	Establishment of the Spanish Inquisition
1481	Ferdinand shares power in Aragon with Isabella
1492	Conquest of Granada and unification of Spain. Jews expelled from Spain. Isabella sponsors Columbus, who discovers America
1495	Annexation of the Canary Islands
1502	Muslims expelled from Spain
1503	Isabella establishes the *Casa de Contratación* to govern the New World
1504	Isabella dies the age of 53

Isabella of Spain—famous for sending Columbus to discover America in 1492—is universally recognized for being extremely pious, for expelling the Jews from Spain, and for instituting the dreadful Spanish Inquisition. However, this single-minded queen also unified Spain and catapulted her country from a medieval backwater into a modern and global power. She was very competent at developing high potentials into effective leaders, able to develop and realize ambitious and inspiring visions, and a fan of innovative technology—just to mention a few of her impressive leadership attributes. But before we explore exactly how Isabella executed her unique brand of leadership and why her example should matter to today's women leaders, let's begin with the most important details from this powerful woman's career (Fig. 3.1).

P. Vanderbroeck, *Leadership Strategies for Women*, Management for Professionals,   25
DOI 10.1007/978-3-642-39623-6_3, © Springer-Verlag Berlin Heidelberg 2014

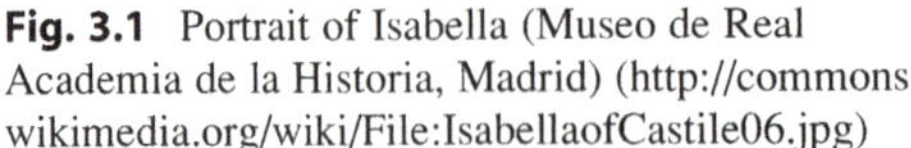

Fig. 3.1 Portrait of Isabella (Museo de Real Academia de la Historia, Madrid) (http://commons. wikimedia.org/wiki/File:IsabellaofCastile06.jpg)

3.1   Life and Career

Isabella I of Spain was born in 1451, the first of two children from the second marriage of Juan, King of Castile, and thus a potential successor to the throne. At this time of the waning of the Middle Ages, the Iberian peninsula was divided into the kingdoms of Castile, Aragon, Portugal, the small kingdom of Navarre, and the Muslim Emirate of Granada. When Isabella was 10 years old, her older half-brother, Enrique IV of Castile, who had succeeded their father as king, brought her to court, where he could keep an eye on his young rival. While there, Isabella received the traditional education of a noble maiden, focusing on literature, the arts, religion, and physical exercise (she became an excellent horsewoman). In 1469, one year after the death of her younger brother, Alfonso, and against Enrique's wishes, Isabella married Ferdinand II of Aragon. Upon Enrique's death 5 years later, Isabella claimed the throne at the age of 23, sparking a civil war with other claimants to the throne that she and Ferdinand successfully quashed in 1476.

Having established their power, the two monarchs set out to realize Isabella's first vision: a unified Spain. They reinforced the authority of the state, reorganized the management structure, recruited talented individuals for key positions, and improved the income of the realm. They also created a new, unified culture, establishing the Spanish Inquisition in 1480 and using it to identify people perceived as disloyal to the national religion. In 1481, Ferdinand declared Isabella his co-ruler of Aragon.

In 1492, following a 10-year campaign, the rulers defeated the Emirate of Granada, thus completing the reunification of Spain. Also that year, Isabella granted her support to Christopher Columbus in his quest to find a westward passage to India in support of Isabella's second vision: overseas expansion. Columbus discovered America.

By the time Isabella died of natural causes in 1504, she was 53 years old and had ruled for 30 years. She and her husband—once the rulers of two midsize medieval kingdoms—had created the foundation for the unified country of Spain, which emerged as a global player boasting an organization that was more advanced than most other competitors.

3.2   Key Leadership Challenges

When Isabella became queen she took on the following challenges:
* Directing her career
* Managing the merger between Castile and Aragon
* Creating and developing a vision and strategy of growth
* Creating the new organization and culture of the unified Spain
* Ensuring her own succession

3.2.1   The Path to Power and Career Management

Isabella started out third in line to the throne, behind Enrique and her younger brother, Alfonso, and she dropped down even further in succession when Enrique had children. Isabella therefore grew up with a keen sense of competition.

Enrique's reign was riddled with power struggles between the king and the aristocracy. When Alfonso died, in 1468, a strong group among the aristocracy urged Isabella to claim the throne. Just 17 years old at the time, Isabella refused. Rather than start a civil war, she chose to capitalize on the rumor that Enrique was not actually the father of his daughter and heir, Juana, and negotiated with him instead. The result was a treaty stipulating that Isabella would replace Juana as Enrique's successor. It further stated that Enrique would settle an estate upon Isabella as a crown princess and gave Enrique the right to veto Isabella's choice of husband.

When Enrique failed to honor his end of the bargain (the estate never materialized), Isabella felt free to negotiate marriage to Ferdinand, then crown prince of Aragon, without Enrique's knowledge in 1469. Upon hearing the news, Enrique immediately disinherited Isabella—but he failed to clearly reinstate Juana as his heir.

Five years later, in 1474, Enrique died. Isabella, without telling Ferdinand who was tending to business in Aragon, immediately seized the throne. On the morning of her coronation, which she carefully staged, she donned a dazzling dress and fine jewelry for the procession. In front of her rode a noble knight, holding up a sword, the symbol of justice. The sword was not the customary symbol of regal power, but Isabella employed it for two reasons: first, to clearly state her royal claim and second, to symbolize what would be new about her reign: law and order. She then crowned herself Queen of Castile.

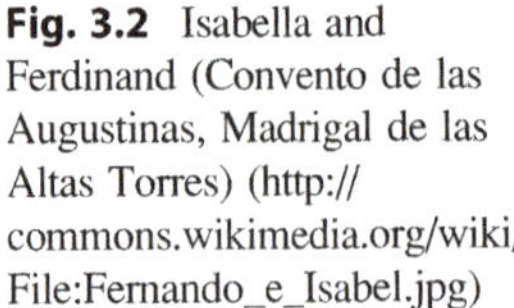

Fig. 3.2 Isabella and Ferdinand (Convento de las Augustinas, Madrigal de las Altas Torres) (http://commons.wikimedia.org/wiki/File:Fernando_e_Isabel.jpg)

Given the dubious legality of Isabella's succession, some members of the aristocracy aligned themselves with Afonso, the king of Portugal, and challenged Isabella on behalf of Juana's claim to the throne. Ferdinand and Isabella quelled the ensuing civil war and confined Juana to a convent for the rest of her life. Isabella's authority was never challenged again.

Isabella's husband was also her team member. Although she picked Ferdinand for his professional abilities and for his heritage, it seems that the two genuinely loved each other. The story about how they first met is remarkably romantic. Ferdinand, then 17 years old and disguised as a merchant to avoid King Enrique's troops, made the perilous voyage to a secret location in Castile to marry the bride he had never met before. Isabella personally nursed Ferdinand back to health, when he was injured. The letters, in which they discussed work issues while in different places, always contained words of love, kindness and concern for each other. Of course, these are the Middle Ages, the most romantic period of history, with its noble knights, fair princesses, minstrels and poetry. Still, it seems the couple's expressions went beyond mere convention (Fig. 3.2).

Ferdinand was notoriously promiscuous. A fact well known to Isabella and a thorn in her eyes, but not a deal-breaker in their marriage. Isabella magnanimously accepted the illegitimate children he had fathered before their marriage at the court. After their marriage, Isabella made sure that Ferdinand's mistresses stayed away from court. Together they had six children, three of which survived their parents. Isabella miscarried at least once, while riding through Spain to rally support for her cause during the civil war. She kept a close watch on the education of her children, hiring excellent teachers from Renaissance Italy, and making sure that the daily program she had designed for them was performed to the letter. Sparks flew regularly between the couple. Yet they seemed to have been mainly about professional matters. And they always reached an agreement.

Isabella put all her hopes of completing her vision of a unified Spain in her son and heir Juan, whom she loved dearly. When he died prematurely, Isabella was at a loss and never really recovered. Isabella seems to have been unhappy during the later years of her life. In 1504, at the age of 53, she drew up her will. She left the throne to her daughter Juana. But because she already had doubts about Juana's mental capacity, she included a clause that gave Ferdinand the power to rule on her behalf, if necessary. Ferdinand did indeed exercise that power as from 1506, when it was determined that Juana was mentally ill.

Isabella's will shows that she was disappointed in the organization she had created: Overhead was too great, too many people were receiving financial grants from the crown, tax collectors were getting too big a cut, judicial reform was proceeding too slowly. In short, Isabella felt that she had created an inefficient management structure. She called upon her successors to make further improvements a priority.

3.2.2   Managing the Merger of Castile and Aragon

Nine months before their wedding, Isabella and Ferdinand signed a prenuptial agreement. The contract spelled out their roles and responsibilities once they ascended to their respective thrones. The *Capitulations of Cervera,* as the stipulations were called, particularly described the boundaries of Ferdinand's authority in Castile. For example, they stated that Ferdinand needed Isabella's permission to declare war or conclude an alliance, to give away royal possessions, and to nominate key staff.

This laying down the law with regard to governance was Isabella's initiative. She needed Ferdinand to reinforce her claim to the throne. At the same time, she knew that she would be putting her sovereignty at risk if she declared Ferdinand the king of Castile. After all, in Castile, women were only allowed to rule in the absence of a suitable man, while in Aragon, where Ferdinand had grown up, women were not allowed to rule under any circumstances. Moreover, Castile was three times the size of Aragon in territory, population, and financial resources. Bringing in the bigger chunk gave Isabella another reason to clarify things up front.

Ferdinand was quite angry when Isabella crowned herself the sole monarch and informed him about the event addressing him as "my lawful husband". Pre-nup aside, he had expected to be named king too and not just consort. Some hefty negotiations followed in Segovia in 1475, leading to an updated contract. The deal ensured that although Ferdinand would not become king, he would figure on all official documents and coins. Furthermore, the coat of arms of Castile and Aragon would be integrated, and the revenues of their kingdoms would be shared. The slogan on the new heraldic arms read *Tanto monta*, which means, "Each is as important as the other." The agreement shows that, at least in Castile, the two monarchs found it important to act as one toward their organization, even though their governing powers differed. Isabella took charge of internal affairs, including finance and logistics, while Ferdinand oversaw foreign and military operations.

When war broke out, following Isabella's initiative to seize the crown, things got awry. Now that it had become a matter of life and death, Isabella felt constrained to grant Ferdinand full powers in Castile, while keeping full ownership of the throne. In 1481, Ferdinand named Isabella joint ruler on the throne of Aragon.

Isabella and Ferdinand wanted to go about the merger in steps, aiming at full unity after their death. They mutually supported each other's projects while

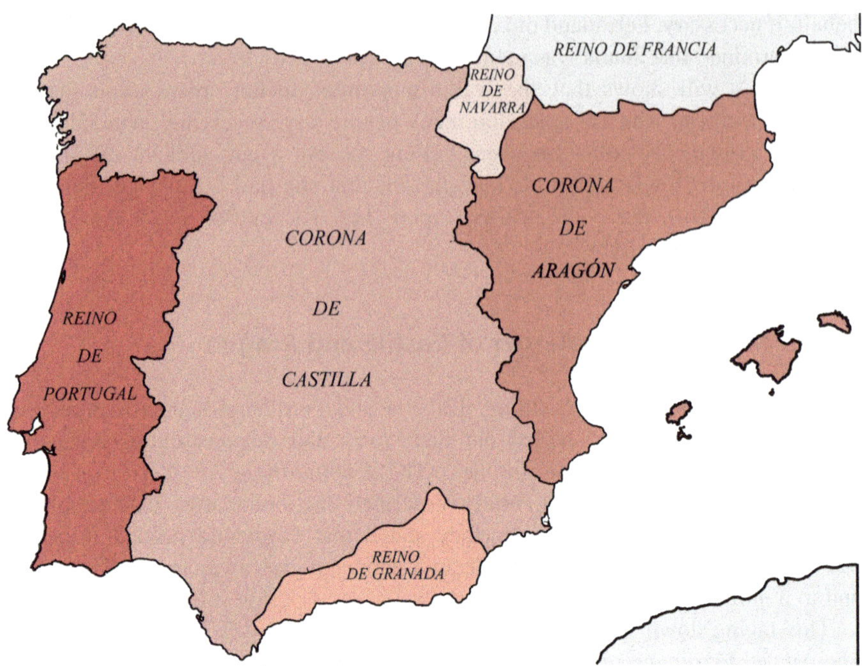

Fig. 3.3 Map of the territories (except Portugal) that Isabella merged into one Spain (http://commons.wikimedia.org/wiki/File:Iberian_Kingdoms_in_1400.svg)

pursuing their own strategies and directions. Since Castile looked south towards the Muslim lands and west across the Atlantic, the reconquest of Granada and the exploration of the New World would be mainly a Castilian undertaking. Aragon, which looked north toward France and east across the Mediterranean, would therefore work on becoming a major player in the Old World. Since Aragon had a more decentralized organization, which made restructuring more difficult, the pragmatic monarchs decided to tackle structural matters in Castile first and in Aragon later.

The deal of Segovia also made clear how Ferdinand and Isabella originally saw the merger unfolding: If Isabella died first, their daughter Isabel, not Ferdinand, would succeed to the throne of Castile. Shortly thereafter, Ferdinand would name Isabel heir to the throne of Aragon as well, despite the laws of succession. So while Isabella and Ferdinand would rule independently, the idea was that their descendant would realize the vision of a united and independent Spain by inheriting and joining the crowns of Castile and Aragon (Fig. 3.3).

3.2.3   Creating and Developing a Vision and Strategy of Growth

Rather than looking for synergies and economies of scale, the added value from the merger came from a joint vision of growth. The completion of the *Reconquista*, or taking back, of Spain from the Muslim invaders had been announced as the joint vision of the crown prince and princess at the time of their marriage. As soon as Isabella's throne in Castile was secure, the two rulers agreed to tackle Granada, the last stretch of Spanish soil under Muslim rule. Isabella approached the task with remarkable single mindedness, even pawning her jewelry to raise money for the army. After 10 years of protracted war, victory was hers in 1492.

After the reconquest of Granada, the couple decided to turn attention towards the Mediterranean. Here Aragon's traditional interests were successfully pursued. The strategy was to isolate France, the biggest competitor, by marital alliances and military campaigns. They acquired Roussillon and Cerdagne to the north of the Pyrenees Mountains, as well as Naples and the south of Italy, thanks to superior military tactics developed in the war against the Moors.

Overseas, Isabella's greatest venture, apart from conquering the Canary Islands in 1495, was sending off Christopher Columbus to explore uncharted territory in 1492. The implications of his initial discoveries were immediately clear to the rulers. Several senior civil servants and missionaries accompanied Columbus on his second expedition to impose royal justice and stake both financial and ideological claims on the discoveries. In 1503, Isabella set up the *Casa de Contratación*, which handled taxation and centralized all permits for trade, shipping, and emigration to the New World. It attests to the fact that both Isabella and Ferdinand realized the need for a fresh approach to management of the new lands and future conquests.

Isabella and Ferdinand's strategy of growth and expansion provided opportunities to gain honor for the higher nobility, career prospects for lesser nobles and ambitious citizens, and treasure for all. As a result, the economy was stimulated and boomed.

3.2.4   Creating the New Culture and Organization of the Unified Spain

To realize their vision, Isabella and Ferdinand worked to create a culture that would support a sustainable, unified Spain, an organizational structure that would facilitate unification, and to provide the resources for implementing this strategy.

The two monarchs started by increasing the effectiveness of already existing institutions—an example of their pragmatic approach: happy to innovate, but only when necessary. Their senior management team, the *Consejo Real*, dealt with critical matters of the realm. The *Santa Hermandad*, a national and centrally run paramilitary organization with judicial powers aimed at establishing law and order and used for collecting taxes, was set up first in Castile and then in Aragon. It proved to be very effective and a key factor in reinforcing the credibility, and thus the authority, of the monarchy.[1]

---

[1] The *consejo* had a functional distribution: Foreign Affairs, Justice, the *Hermandad*, Finance, the Kingdom of Aragon. Later the department of Inquisition was added. The *consejo* had 12 members: 3 knights and 9 lawyers.

To reinforce central authority even further, Isabella and Ferdinand gained permission from Pope Sixtus IV to appoint bishops and other senior clergy in Spain and the New World. This gave them a strong influence in religious matters and access to the wealth of the church. Perhaps more important, however, it also provided them with a counterbalancing power to the aristocracy, because bishops at the time ruled like noblemen over vast territories. In all other regards, Aragon and Castile were not fully merged, but ruled as something akin to a federation by the two monarchs.

Isabella and Ferdinand took several significant steps to forge a single and strong organizational culture. First, they caused the existing laws of Castile to be written up in a compendium (*Ordenanzas Reales de Castilla*), copied via the printing press, and then distributed to every town. By doing so, Isabella ensured a standard application of policies by all parts of the organization.

Next, in a truly innovative move, came the *Gramática Castellana*, which was the first grammar book of any European language and was dedicated to the Queen. Its author—Antonio de Nebrija—noted that the development of a language goes hand in hand with power. Isabella's confessor, the monk Hernando de Talavera, explained to the queen how such a book could aid the integration of conquered lands by accelerating the native peoples' ability to learn Castilian and thus understand Spanish laws.

Third, once Granada had been reclaimed, the monarchs banned the use of the Arabic language. The legal compendium, the grammar, the printing press and the ban on the use of Arabic reinforced establishing a single language to be used as an effective instrument of power.

Earlier in their reign, in 1480, the two leaders took perhaps the boldest step to create a society that shared their vision, was loyal, and worked in accordance to the same norms and values. Believing that the presence of other ideas on Spanish soil would prevent their new value system from taking hold, they took radical measures to irradiate those ideas. To accomplish that task, they established the Spanish Inquisition.

The Spanish Inquisition was meant to identify and condemn false converts to Christianity. The outcome was a series of public trials, not unlike the twentieth century show trials of the former Communist world, which uncovered and executed both real and false converts. As a result, all Jews were expelled from Spain in 1492 and all Muslims were expelled 10 years later. The defining criterion in these trials was loyalty to the new culture. Many Jewish converts remained among the most important members of the royal staff, and expelled Jews who later converted were permitted to return and get their goods back.[2]

The royal couple knew that particularly the measure of the expulsion of the Jews was controversial, and they wanted to make sure that it had a positive effect on the

---

[2] Talavera, monk and Isabella's CFO and confessor, was half-Jewish for example. However, as he also was a critic of the Inquisition, he was put on trial by the Inquisition later in his life, but acquitted.

organizational culture. They took the measure after careful reflection and deliberation with their counselors. Reaching an understanding with the "survivors" of this "downsizing" operation, i.e. the remainder of the country, therefore, was of importance. They explained their reasons and step-by-step approach at great length in the decree ordering the expulsion of the Jews. With these measures, their power over the clergy, and their insistence in appointing only Spanish nationals to church positions, Isabella and Ferdinand essentially established a national religion.

Was all this necessary in order to realize Isabella's vision of a unified Spain? The state religion to create a single value system probably was; the Inquisition and the expulsion of the Jews for certain were not. An important part of the exiled Jews eventually ended up in Amsterdam. Not only did they provide a key contribution to the economic, academic and artistic bloom of the Netherlands in the seventeenth century. But also they managed to do so under a state religion (Calvinism) that was as ideologically intolerant as Isabella's. The difference being that the Netherlands already then started its famous practice of tolerance of difference, as long as it does not interfere with law and order.

Finally, pragmatism, rather than innovation, was the norm when it came to resource management as well. Isabella had inherited a rather messy financial system in Castile, so she set about reducing the financial privileges of the aristocracy, which sapped the royal coffers. The crown also took back authority over the knightly orders and their rich possessions. In addition, the monarchs used every opportunity to extract even more revenue through taxation. Using a variety of both regular and exceptional measures, Isabella and Ferdinand were able to double the tax revenue for the crown during their reign. At the same time, however, their expenditure, e.g. as a result of the growing overhead of their central government, grew even more.

3.3   Key Leadership Competencies

3.3.1   Vision and Strategy Development

Isabella's choice of Ferdinand for a husband shows that she had developed her vision of creating a unified and strong Spain long before ascending the throne. And when it came time to begin merging Castile with Aragon, she chose to do so through expansion rather than through "synergies" or economies of scale. After all, increasing the realm meant more opportunities for all. Her single mindedness almost got the better of the plan, however. Isabella put all her eggs in one basket by counting on particular successors to fully merge the two entities. Though the strategy was completed after Isabella's death, it could easily have failed for lack of a successor.

Her second vision, overseas expansion into uncharted territory, was a bold follow-up of the first. Isabella may not have known that Columbus would find a new continent. But given that the Portuguese had been adding discovery to discovery around that time—Bartolomeu Dias had rounded the Cape of Good Hope shortly before Isabella called Columbus back in for talks—it was reasonable to expect that he would stumble onto something if he looked hard enough. And once the discovery was made, she put a management system in place for the government and colonization that would form the basis of Spain's economic power in centuries to come.

Once Isabella set her mind on something, she was determined to achieve it, no matter how. Her choice of Ferdinand for a husband shows her willingness to achieve her vision of a unified Spain, which she pursued relentlessly. The new coat of arms the royal couple designed also gives us a glimpse of the personal leadership styles of the two monarchs. Isabella brought in bound arrows, which can be interpreted as a set of actions that reinforce each other in attaining a joint purpose. That seems very true to Isabella's nature, who pursued a number of strategies—military, economic, financial, cultural, and structural—for realizing the vision of unified Spain. Ferdinand brought in the Gordian knot, cut by the sword, and his slogan *tanto monta*. The cutting of the Gordian knot by Alexander the Great as an alternative to untying it, symbolizes pragmatism. So, *tanto monta*, apart from implying "it does not matter *who*", i.e. Isabella or Ferdinand, also implies "it does not matter *how*".

Both monarchs were highly pragmatic, so much so in fact that Ferdinand gained Machiavelli's admiration. Despite several power struggles with Ferdinand, Isabella was willing to share control with him in 1475, once that seemed key to winning the war for the throne in Castile. And in 1492, Isabella and Ferdinand agreed to unusually mild terms for the capitulation of Granada and other towns in order to limit costs and loss of life (Fig. 3.4).

3.3.2 Generating Positive Change

Isabella never let boundaries stand in the way of achieving her goals. For example, she had to get a papal dispensation to marry Ferdinand because she was related to him through her grandfather.

Isabella's reign offers a powerful lesson in change management. She and her husband first worked on cultural alignment of the organization before tackling its structure. In modern mergers, things usually happen the other way around, which often means that people begin working in a structure for which their mindset is not yet ripe. Isabella and Ferdinand first created a common value system, in the form of a national religion; then established a joint purpose (the reconquest of the territories remaining in Muslim hands); and finally ensured a strong presence of the two top leaders as a symbol of unity. They reinforced this by introducing three important structural measures to the entire organization: obtaining power over the appointment of the clergy, establishing the Spanish Inquisition, and using the *Santa Hermandad* as a national police force. Thus they laid the groundwork for their successor to easily unify the organizational structure into a single state.

How did Isabella cope with the gender bias she faced? She pushed the boundaries in Castile. Not only did she retain her power despite being married, but instead of naming her husband as heir to the throne, she named her daughter

Fig. 3.4 Isabella and Ferdinand's Coat of arms with their slogan and the symbols of the Gordian knot and the bundled arrows (http://commons.wikimedia.org/wiki/File:Coat_of_Arms_of_Queen_Isabella_of_Castile_(1492–1504).svg)

Isabel. Nevertheless, she did follow conventional rules when the couple's son, Juan, was born, allowing him to trump his sister in succession. Was this a regression on Isabella's part? Possibly. In any case, her daughter's claim was sacrificed in the grander scheme of things. Interestingly, Ferdinand had also flouted his country's laws of succession by agreeing to name Isabel heir to the throne of Aragon as well. His contravention was even more egregious than Isabella's because the Aragonese law of succession prohibited female rulers altogether. He even went so far as to call for the abolition of that law, install Isabella as co-ruler in Aragon, and get the Aragonese parliament to ratify his daughter's claim to the throne. Yet even so, he, too, went along with favoring the son over the elder sister when Juan was born.

Ferdinand, it appears, was willing to push the boundaries of gender discrimination further than Isabella, who was more concerned with unifying Spain than changing Castilian succession laws. And she knew that her vision would be realized by the heir who would meet the least resistance. Machiavelli mentioned Ferdinand as an example of an effective ruler. It seems Isabella was at least as Machiavellian as her husband.

Still, Isabella could have done better. Because her strategy depended on a successor to realize the vision, Isabella faced the possibility of defeat when several of her succession candidates (her son, a daughter, and a grandson) died. Two of her married daughters remained possible successors, but given that they were married to the kings of England and Portugal, respectively, Isabella was reluctant to put her country's independence at risk by choosing either one of them. As she did not expect to need to put them on the succession list, she apparently had not advised her daughters to conclude a prenuptial agreement such as their mother's. Isabella could have used the last years of her reign to accelerate the structural unification of Spain to compensate for a unifying person at the helm. But that would have required an organizational set-up along the lines of a *Magna Carta*, which constrained the monarch's powers, and that was clearly a boundary she did not want to push. Letting go of control as a top leader was unthinkable for her.

Though the strategy to create a unified organizational culture in preparation of a structural merger did bear fruit, it was not without cost. The Inquisition certainly helped—more by force than by conviction—to create a single value system in Spain. So did the expulsion of Jews and Muslims. But the country lost untold amounts of skills and talent as a result.

Both Isabella and Ferdinand put technology to good use to support their change projects. Isabella used the relatively new invention of the printing press in several ways: to communicate messages, enforce the use of standard policies, and for financial management. The monarchs also propelled Spain into a seafaring nation on the world's oceans by leveraging new developments in maritime technology. And they used artillery as a determining weapon in the campaign against Granada.

3.3.3 Leveraging Difference

How did Isabella deal with being considered a second-choice ruler according to law and custom in Castile? In the years leading up to her reign, Isabella received some support. An Augustinian friar, Martin de Cordoba, wrote a treatise in her honor, countering arguments against female rule. He argued that a queen's power derives from her roles as the merciful mother, protector, and advocate of her people. She may be compared to the Virgin Mary, regarded as a daughter of kings and as man's representative in heaven. As a young queen, Isabella asked her confessor, Talavera, for spiritual guidance. Talavera wrote a sermon for her that encouraged her to act as a parent toward her subjects and exhorted her to strive for the virtues of humility and compassion imbued in the "Virgin Mary, Queen of Heaven." Other authors, of course, have criticized female rule.

Isabella was astute at exploiting the archetype of the Virgin Mary, who herself actually combines two archetypes: (1) the nurturing, protective mother (like Hera (Juno) in Greco-Roman mythology and Isis in Egyptian mythology) and (2) the virgin, who holds the moral high ground and sometimes is the stern teacher (like Pallas Athena (Minerva) in Greco-Roman mythology).[3] Isabella used those archetypes differently over time. Up until 1492, she was almost constantly at war, first to secure her throne, then to complete the *Reconquista*. During that time, the

---

[3] Indeed, as Renaissance Humanism came to Spain in the same period, Isabella was compared to Athena.

mother archetype prevailed: she nurtured her people by, for example, establishing the first military hospital in history, tax exemptions for the families of the dead and wounded, and organizing the financial resources to pay for the war.

Another, especially interesting, example of the mother archetype occurred during the first year of the civil war. After Ferdinand abandoned a siege for the town of Toro, Isabella sternly and publicly admonished him and his troops. It was unusual for a woman to openly criticize a male leader, but Isabella felt entitled to do so because, as she reminded them, she had at least as much to lose as they did, namely her husband, her knights, and her wealth. Ferdinand, also publicly, expressed surprise that Isabella had met them with scorn instead of encouragement and consolation, but he promised to do better in the future nevertheless (though he did complain that *women always are so dissatisfied*[4]). Isabella's reaction proved to be effective not because she adopted male behavior but because she used the archetype of the demanding mother: She was caring, but she had high expectations of her "children." Ferdinand's response was an expression of his frustration about not performing up to her standards.

The virgin archetype became apparent during times of peace and when fighting took place beyond Spain's borders. Isabella took great care to avoid any hint of impropriety in her behavior. For example, when traveling without her husband, she slept surrounded by her ladies to ensure no cause for rumor. She also publicly displayed her religious devotion by sponsoring the building of churches and monasteries as well as works of art and literature on Christ and Christian life. Her contemporaries, including her husband, considered her to be a shining example of piety. And it was thanks to her that she and her husband received the honorific title of *los reyes Católicos* (the Catholic Kings).

Isabella's behavior was constantly scrutinized in light of her gender, sometimes with approval and sometimes not. For example, she was favorably compared to successful male warriors and kings: In one set of poems, written on the occasion of the military campaign against Granada, Isabella was even described as a knight as great at *El Cid*.[5] On the other hand, however, Isabella was criticized for displaying the sword, considered a male symbol, at her coronation. But was the sword a symbol of masculinity itself or rather a symbol of power that was strongly associated with men because they had held the top job thus far? More likely, the latter. Isabella's main concern was eliminating any question about who was in charge, particularly since she had married Ferdinand.

Yet she was careful to balance her role as queen with her role as Ferdinand's wife. For instance, she publicly portrayed herself as equal to her husband when in fact she had more power than he did. She also sewed Ferdinand's shirts with her own hands and instructed her daughters in prayers and needlework.

---

[4] Edwards 15–16; Liss 118–119.

[5] The contemporary chronicler Fernando del Pulgar said that *what many men and great lords did not manage to do in many years, a single woman did in a short time through work and governance.*: Liss xi.

Once established on the throne and after having demonstrated an impressive track record, the consensus among her contemporaries was that she was an extraordinary leader. Incidentally, she inspired the major change in the rules of chess that coincided with her reign and through which the queen became the most powerful piece in the game.

3.3.4   Talent Management

Isabella surrounded herself with talented individuals right from the start, beginning with Ferdinand (for it was she who selected him and not the other way around). Aragon represented the largest slice of Spain after Castile and therefore was a logical match for Isabella's vision of a unified Spain. Ferdinand's skills—an education in foreign affairs and military training as a medieval knight—were equally important, however. Once they started working together, their mutual appreciation, and perhaps love, for each other grew.

In modern terms, Isabella and Ferdinand established a "high-potential pool": They recorded the names of talented people in all levels of society who would be suitable candidates for management positions in the government and the church. They also introduced a type of management trainee program, where they actively recruited law graduates, who then had the opportunity to rise to senior positions in the royal administration and the clergy. Those *letrados*, as they were called, went on to become key factors in the professionalization of the management of the realm. Even Isabella's military hospital demonstrates her interest in taking care of skilled staff: It was more efficient to get wounded soldiers to fight again than to recruit and train new ones.

In 1480, the monarchs issued a talent management policy: Management jobs would be awarded only to the best candidates, who would have to have completed at least 10 years of legal studies, and they would no longer be passed down from father to son. In 1601, Juan de Mariana, a Spanish historian, put it thus:

> *What really deserves praise is that they distributed prizes and honors (. . .) not based on the nobility of one's ancestors or on some personal favor, bur rather based on each person's merits, thus inspiring the talents of their vassals and leading them to devote themselves to the pursuit of virtue and learning. So much good came of this that one cannot even describe it.*[6]

Many exemplars abound of Isabella's skill in choosing and developing talented individuals with a penchant for innovation. Christopher Columbus is perhaps the most well known. Another of the Queen's protégés was Gonzalo Fernández de Córdoba, a soldier who made his mark in the war against Granada. He grew into the greatest military genius and innovator of the age and was the principal architect of Spain's victory over France in Italy, despite inferior resources. Diego de Valera, a Jewish convert, provided Isabella and Ferdinand with advice on how to innovate

---

[6]"Juan de Mariana, The Conquest of Granada (1601)", in Cowans 13.

their military strategy by combining the operations of land and naval forces in order to win the war against Granada. And, of course, there was Talavera, who in addition to being Isabella's confessor, was also a financial expert.

Isabella put an emphasis on learning. She sponsored the University of Salamanca, Spain's oldest and foremost academic institution, which became a key recruiting ground for staff members. She also led by example in this matter: Since she had missed out on learning Latin as a child, she took lessons as an adult.

3.3.5 Giving and Receiving Feedback

Isabella was an assertive woman. Her bold move in marrying Ferdinand without her brother's approval is one testament to that. Another concerns the part of the dowry that Ferdinand's father had granted Isabella: a rental income from Sicily. She protested vehemently when Ferdinand's father assigned a representative to manage the income without her involvement.

At the same time, she appreciated people who had the courage to speak truth to power. In fact, both she and her husband appreciated mutual candor and feedback from one another. It was a key factor in the success of their teamwork. Isabella took Talavera as her first confessor and close adviser after he had refused to kneel for her, claiming to be God's representative on Earth. He was also chosen to write up Ferdinand's will despite the negative feedback he'd offered on the king's behavior. When Talavera left to become the first bishop of Granada, Isabella named a new confessor, Francisco de Cisneros, Archbishop of Toledo. Cisneros, to the delight of the Queen, told her she was a mortal just like him. The two monarchs also appreciated the candor of Fernando de Zafra, their royal secretary, who told them that it was impossible to uphold the mild terms of Granada's surrender and create economic growth in the new territories by inviting Christian settlers.

By appreciating others' candor, the Queen prevented her own assertiveness from turning into arrogance. But the downside is that Isabella could overvalue the advice of opinionated people. Since she was clear in what she wanted, she appreciated the same thing in others. She probably had little time for nuance and ambiguity. So while she sponsored a gutsy guy like Columbus, she also favored extremists, such as Chief Inquisitor Torquemada, the Pol Pot of the Middle Ages.[7]

3.3.6 Communication

Immediately after Enrique named Isabella the heir to his throne, she started to write letters to stakeholders, such as nobles, church leaders, and town councils. She passed on information about herself and asked for advice. And when Isabella and Ferdinand were apart, which happened often, they communicated via fast couriers

---

[7] Torquemada, unsurprisingly, was also one of the advisers pushing for expulsion of the Jews.

carrying letters. Isabella knew how to put some oomph into her communication, too: At her self-staged coronation in 1475, her royal garb and the symbol of power she chose spoke volumes. And her public dressing-down of Ferdinand and his army when they abandoned the siege of Toro was also highly effective.

The two monarchs took public relations very seriously. To show themselves equal and unified towards their organization, for example, they ate together in the public hall and had visibly pleasant conversations. Their slogan, *Tanto monta, monta tanto, Isabel como Fernando* (which also translates to "one is worth as much as the other—Isabel like Fernando") was represented in short form on their coat of arms and published widely on coins, seals, tapestries, and public buildings. And rather than remain isolated in a capital, the court travelled around the country in a medieval road show, offering public performance by their court musicians and staging chivalric tournaments.

When Ferdinand and the army marched off to war to defend Isabella's crown, she was there, clearly visible from a hilltop to encourage the troops with her words and cheerful smile. In the war against Granada, Isabella often appeared prominently at the front lines to boost morale. And she made certain that military victories were communicated and celebrated throughout the kingdom. Generally the monarchs' entry into any given city was a spectacle, once even involving an elephant.

When the printing press was introduced in Spain 4 years after Isabella came to power, she immediately grasped its importance. To encourage its use, she exempted the new machine from taxation, and she used it actively herself to publish laws and statements.

Thus Isabella proved to be a master of internal communication through letters, staged public appearances, a powerful slogan, distribution of visual imagery and symbols, and the active use of the printing press. Her efforts ensured that her vision of a unified Spain was easily adopted by the entire organization. At the same time, however, the dark side of the realization of these visions, such as the Inquisition, was more easily adopted too.

3.4 Isabella's Leadership Impact

Isabella was the first monarch to propel her kingdom from the Middle Ages into the modern era. Whereas Ferdinand was a classic late-medieval monarch, focused on wheeling, dealing, and competing with other kings. Spain was the first European country to have a national church, a centralized and professional state, and an economy built on trade and empire. Other nations subsequently followed, beginning with England. Henry VIII's establishment of the Church of England had a similar impact on his subjects' religion as Isabella's right to appoint bishops had on hers. The principle of *cuius regio, eius religio*—the notion that the head of state determines the national religion—swept through Europe shortly thereafter.

Yet Isabella with the Inquisition and the expulsion of the Jews and Muslims took it to extremes.

Isabella and her husband established a highly effective coregency under equal terms. They supported each other in accordance with their joint motto. Without Isabella, Spain's unification would have taken much longer, and other European nations would have taken center stage. And while America would certainly have been discovered at some point, it might well have been colonized from the north instead.

3.5   What Women Can Learn from This Leader

Based on the discussion above, we come to the following performance appraisal and leadership assessment of Isabella.

Leadership Challenge	Rating
Career Direction	Fully Achieved
Managing the merger between Castile and Aragon	Fully Achieved
Vision and strategy of growth	Fully Achieved
Succession Management	Partially Achieved
Renewing Organizational Culture	Fully Achieved

Leadership Competency	Rating
Vision and Strategy Development	Strong
Generating Positive Change	Competent
Leveraging Difference	Strong
Talent Management	Strong
Giving and Receiving Feedback	Competent
Communication	Strong

Isabella had no real flaws in her competencies. Everything that was under her control operated smoothly, and she ultimately overcame any resistance she encountered. In the end, however, that became an overused strength. Since Isabella never really experienced defeat, she never learned how to deal with it. At the same time the struggle to get on the throne plus the bias against a female ruler may have left her fundamentally insecure. Isabella never came up with an alternative way of realizing the vision of unification other than through an heir to the throne; she faced failure with the death of each subsequent succession candidate. Put differently, it was impossible for this "superwoman" to envision any way of doing something other than her own way of central rule. If her grandson Charles V had not taken up the legacy several years after Isabella's death, the grand plan would have fallen into shambles.

Realizing a vision means implementing change. Isabella proved to be an effective change manager, willing to push boundaries to create a new organization with a strong culture. Creating the new culture before creating the new structure was a smart approach. Yet she stopped short of applying change to her own concept of leadership, when that was asked for.

Isabella's ability to give and receive feedback was a strong asset in pushing through the change needed to realize her visions. Yet putting too much value on opinionated people made her sometimes follow extreme rather than nuanced advice. Her communication, another strong competency meets a similar assessment: effective and innovative in supporting both sensible and extremist ideas. Isabella realized the results she wanted by setting challenging objectives and by favoring the *what* over the *how*. Yet that approach also had a dark side: She ruthlessly isolated her cousin and rival to the throne, Juana, as well as broke treaties once they were no longer to her advantage.

Her self-evaluation was a bit harsh, though. Isabella's achievements, both in relation to the goals she set out at the beginning of her career and to the opportunities she grasped along the way, are undeniable. And she must have received plenty of positive feedback from people whose straightforward opinions she valued, especially Ferdinand. What caused her disappointment? Was it the tendency, often found among women leaders, to underestimate their own achievements? Or was it guilt, which many career women feel, because of the personal sacrifices she had to make in exchange for professional success? Did she perhaps think she did not take care enough of her children? Or perhaps, despite her bravery and stamina, Isabella was a profoundly insecure person.

Unlike Ferdinand, she not only had to fight her way to the throne, but she also had to overcome discrimination against being a woman ruler. She may have even, deep down, felt like an impostor. Whatever she was feeling, she did take control of things and set clear boundaries in both her professional life, as can be seen in her power-sharing contracts with Ferdinand, and in the education of her children. She could not, however, control her children's life expectancy, and her inability to prevent the premature deaths of her children and grandchildren may have been too much for her. This need for control, this need to be "superwoman," is not uncommon with career women. Rather than controlling everything it would have been helpful to plan for more than one contingency and find ways to delegate responsibilities.

And then there was Ferdinand. One lesson Isabella provides is that it pays to pick your life partner well. Ferdinand shared Isabella's life project, both professionally and personally. Not that their partnership was an easy ride. The couple went through many disputes, tough negotiations and contained explosive emotional material. They both had to swallow their pride occasionally, because they realized that together they could achieve more. The couple's slogan *Tanto monta, Isabella como Fernando* can also mean: "we're in this together."

For inspiration to modern women leaders, three competencies come to the fore as Isabella's core strengths. First, she demonstrated that women leaders could be visionaries, just like men. What's more, she did so by developing and realizing two equally ambitious and inspiring visions.

Second, she went about selecting and developing talent in a systematic way. Isabella's experience proves the point that a vision is only as good as the talent required for its realization. She went for quality rather than upbringing in a society where opportunities and rewards were customarily based on social status, not merit. She led by example when it came to self-development. Working effectively in a team with Ferdinand, she demonstrated the power of extending relationships beyond the professional and into the personal.

Third, Isabella effectively leveraged her differences as a woman by exploiting several positive female archetypes, and she successfully fought against the bias of being considered second best. At the same time, she was very aware of what her combined public roles of queen, wife, and mother required, and so her reputation did not suffer. Isabella had a remarkable impact on her contemporaries.

3.6   Top Five Do's and Don'ts from Isabella of Spain

- Do
    - Develop an inspiring and ambitious vision
    - Find a life partner, who is willing and able to support your career
    - Pay attention to the selection and development of your team members
    - Fight for your job in the face of competition
    - Turn your difference as a woman into an opportunity
- Don't
    - Listen more to people who look like you.
    - Be too single minded; you may leave victims along the way.
    - Try to control everything
    - Be intolerant of other beliefs and cultures
    - Be too inflexible in your thinking

Bibliography

Cowans, J. (Ed.). (2003). *Early modern Spain. A documentary history*. Philadelphia: University of Pennsylvania Press.

Edwards, J. (2005). *Ferdinand and Isabella profiles in power*. Harlow: Pearson Longman.

Goldberg, H. (1974). *Jardin de Nobles Donzellas, Fray Martin de Cordoba: A critical edition and study*. Chapel Hill, NC: University of North Carolina.

Gottschalk, M. (2008). *Königinnen. Fünf Herrscherinnen und ihre Lebensgeschichten*. Weinheim: Beltz & Gelberg.

Jansen, S. L. (2002). *The monstrous regiment of Women. Female rulers in early modern Europe*. New York: Palgrave Macmillan.

Ladero, M. A. (1992). *Das Spanien der katholischen Könige. Ferdinand von Aragon und Isabella von Kastilien 1469–1516*. Innsbruck: Haymon-Verlag.

Liss, P. K. (1992). *Isabel the queen: Life and times*. New York: Oxford University Press.

Pérez, J. (1989). *Ferdinand und Isabella. Spanien zur Zeit der Katholischen Könige*. Callwey: München.

Weissberger, B. F. (2004). *Isabel rules: Constructing queenship, wielding power*. Minneapolis, MN: University of Minnesota Press.

Elizabeth I of England: Managing a Team of Men

4

Elizabeth I TIMETABLE

1533	Birth of Elizabeth, daughter of King Henry VIII and his second wife Anne Boleyn
1536	Anne Boleyn, Elizabeth' mother, beheaded at the orders of her father, Henry VIII
1542	Mary Stuart, still an infant, becomes Queen of Scots
1547	Death of King Henry VIII
1547–1553	Governance of Edward Seymour on behalf of King Edward VI, Elizabeth' half-brother, still a boy
1549	Elizabeth suspected of involvement in a plot against King Edward VI
1553–1558	Reign of Elizabeth' half-sister, Mary Tudor as Queen of England. Persecutions of Protestants earn her the nickname of *Bloody Mary*
1554	Elizabeth, suspected of plotting against Queen Mary Tudor, imprisoned in the Tower of London and later under house arrest
1558	Elizabeth I, age 25, crowned Queen of England, following the death of Mary Tudor
1559	Act of Supremacy; Elizabeth named head of the Church of England
1560	Military intervention in Scotland to oust the French troops. Currency reform of the English Pound
1562	Military intervention in France in support of the Protestants
1566	Opening of the London Stock Exchange
1567	Mary Stuart removed from the throne in Scotland in favor of her son James. Mary takes refuge in England
1569–1570	The Northern Earls follow the Duke of Norfolk in rebellion
1577–1580	Francis Drake sails around the globe
1585	Foundation of Virginia, the first English colony in the Americas
1585	Military intervention in the Low Countries to support the Dutch revolt against Spain
1587	Execution of Mary, Queen of Scots, for attempting to overthrow Elizabeth
1588	Spanish Armada unsuccessfully tries to invade England
1588	Leicester dies
1599–1603	Irish rebellion
1601	Execution of Exeter
1603	Elizabeth dies at the age of 69

P. Vanderbroeck, *Leadership Strategies for Women*, Management for Professionals,
DOI 10.1007/978-3-642-39623-6_4, © Springer-Verlag Berlin Heidelberg 2014

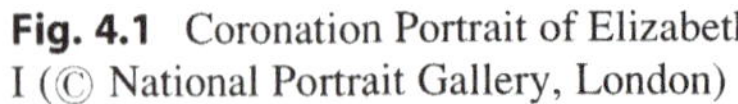

Fig. 4.1 Coronation Portrait of Elizabeth I (© National Portrait Gallery, London)

Elizabeth I—celebrated for saving England from the Spanish Armada in 1588—is universally recognized for being the virgin queen who refused to marry, for the cultural refinement of the Elizabethan era of which Shakespeare is but one example, and for being the nemesis of Mary Queen of Scots. However, this enigmatic queen also laid the foundation for the unique combination of entrepreneurship and insularity that would allow Great Britain over time to grow into a world power. She was masterful at leveraging her difference as a woman in a professional environment full of men, highly skilled at communicating her message to create a followership, and competent at giving feedback at different levels and in a way that was both clear and easy to digest—just to mention a few of her impressive leadership attributes. But before we investigate precisely how Elizabeth executed her unique brand of leadership and why her example should matter to today's women leaders, let's begin with some key dates and facts about this enthralling leader's path to power (Fig'. 4.1).

4.1   Life and Career

Elizabeth Tudor was born in 1533. The daughter of King Henry VIII, Elizabeth succeeded her half-sister Mary I—the infamous Bloody Mary—to the throne at the age of 25. Elizabeth was the second woman to rule England in her own right, and she ruled until her death in 1603 for a total of 44 years.

Elizabeth had an excellent education: She developed sharp critical thinking skills through her study of the classics and Protestant Reformers and became fluent in six languages. She also enjoyed chivalrous tournaments, blood sports, and hunting. Elizabeth became queen as part of a conventional succession plan: Henry VIII's will had put her third in the line of succession after her half-siblings, Edward and Mary, who both ascended to the throne and then died without issue.

Elizabeth inherited a realm destabilized by religious strife, a bad economy, and war with France. In 1564, Elizabeth ended the war, sold Calais to France, and used the money to pay off England's debts. She also reversed Mary's reinstatement of Catholicism and restored the independent Church of England that her father had created.

Though England was inevitably drawn into the religious conflicts raging in Europe, particularly in France and the Netherlands, Elizabeth tried to avoid full-scale war. She preferred to support the Protestant cause with money, sending troops only occasionally. When Catholic Spain dispatched its Armada to England in 1588, however, Elizabeth had no choice but to defend her country with every resource available. Her navy, aided by inclement weather, defeated the Armada and thwarted the invasion of England. Nevertheless, Spain remained a major threat to England throughout Elizabeth's reign.

During the 11 years between her father's death and her own coronation, Elizabeth witnessed several foiled coups d'état against Edward and Mary, and once Queen Elizabeth found that she, too, had to constantly watch her back.

The last decade of Elizabeth's reign was characterized by economic difficulties, resulting from the costs of war against Spain and poor harvests. Elizabeth also had to crush a major revolt in Ireland, keen on freedom from the English yoke. She never married and left no offspring. Her cousin James (the son of Mary Stuart, Queen of Scots) succeeded her. Despite the economic challenges she faced, however, Elizabeth left England better equipped for the future than when she had ascended the throne almost half a century earlier.

4.2 Key Leadership Challenges

When Elizabeth became queen, she took on the following challenges:
- Directing her career;
- Ensuring her own succession;
- Moving her country from loss to profit;
- Dealing with the competition; and
- Renewing the organizational culture.

4.2.1 The Path to Power and Career Management

Elizabeth's path to power was not straightforward. Third in line for the throne, Elizabeth grew up with only a marginal expectation of becoming queen someday, and she realized that her prospects would dwindle even further if her brother or sister produced offspring.

There was little love lost between Elizabeth and her half-sister Mary Tudor. Mary was a staunch Roman Catholic, while Elizabeth adhered to the ideas of the Reformation. Under Mary's rule, Elizabeth showed her political astuteness by publicly attending mass as was required, thereby not giving Mary any reason to move against her. Still, Mary suspected her of supporting Protestant rebels. Consequently, Elizabeth spent almost a year under house arrest, after a short imprisonment in the Tower of London.

When both Edward and Mary Tudor died without issue, Elizabeth became lawfully queen. Elizabeth had prepared herself for the eventuality, since Mary's chances of producing offspring—she was still childless at age 38—had diminished. In her first speech to the court, only a few days after having been declared queen, she articulated concrete, well-developed ideas about how she would work with the leadership team she intended to put together.

Holding on to power was not a straightforward task, either. Elizabeth successfully suppressed several plots and rebellions against her position. Of them all, the threat posed by the other Mary, Queen of Scots and Elizabeth' cousin, may have been the most challenging. Nine years younger than Elizabeth, Mary had become queen of Scotland shortly after her birth in 1542. Tossed off the throne in 1567, she fled to England seeking asylum. Elizabeth didn't know what to do. She was torn between providing refuge for her cousin and fellow monarch on the one hand and potentially harboring a dangerous rival on the other—Mary refused to give up her claim to the English throne and was involved in rebellions against Elizabeth. Sending Mary back to France where she had grown up, however, could risk inviting a French army to Scotland. Elizabeth ultimately decided to place Mary under house arrest, which lasted for almost 20 years. After one too many of Mary's plots, however, Elizabeth stopped dithering about whether to sign Mary's death warrant and finally had her executed, in 1587. Conscious that the execution could have negative repercussions abroad and could be exploited by her Catholic enemies, Elizabeth granted Mary a state funeral.

Elizabeth never married. Unhappy experiences from her youth reinforced her negative views toward marriage: Her father had ordered the execution of her mother, Ann Boleyn. Her stepfather had abused her when she was 14 years old. Yet Elizabeth clearly struggled with her decision to stay single. Early in her reign, still in her twenties, she became close to Robert Dudley, the dashing Earl of Leicester. The two flirted publicly, and her entourage thought she was in love. For a while, they even had adjacent bedrooms. Leicester for sure had his hopes up about marrying the Queen, but Elizabeth had little intention of doing so. Her leadership team strongly advised against it because they considered the rank of earl to be too low for the Queen's consort (Fig. 4.2).

Later, Elizabeth entered into a courtship with François, Duke of Alençon brother of the King of France and exchanged love letters with him. However, she broke off the relationship because she did not want to contemplate marriage. Then, when she

Fig. 4.2 Portrait of Robert Dudley, Earl of Leicester (© National Portrait Gallery, London)

was in her 50s, Elizabeth enjoyed the attentions of Robert Devereux, the Earl of Essex—who was 34 years her junior—and lavished him with favors.

Despite her many suitors, Elizabeth became forever known as the Virgin Queen because she never married. Whether or not Elizabeth actually remained a virgin throughout her life, however, is still a mystery.

The consequence of Elizabeth's decision to remain single was that her personal and professional lives merged together. Thus the most incompetent members of her otherwise capable leadership team were able to curry favor, and Elizabeth's objectivity and performance management both suffered badly. At the end of the day she faced her decisions alone.

4.2.2 Ensuring Her Own Succession

Succession is a leadership challenge that every person at the top has to meet, and it was a point of particular contention throughout Elizabeth's reign. For the Queen, developing a successor meant producing a legitimate heir, and that implied marriage. Furthermore, any potential husband she chose was subject to Parliament's approval. Marriage, therefore was a recurrent topic of discussion. And just as when she had ascended to the throne, Elizabeth made up her mind and prepared herself well for the question.

As princess, she resisted pressure from her half-sister, Mary I, to be married off to some continental Catholic prince. And as queen she felt that she was married to the job. In an early speech,[1] Elizabeth said:

But when the public charge of governing the kingdom came upon me, it seemed unto me an inconsiderate folly to draw upon myself the cares which might proceed of marriage. To conclude, I am already bound unto an husband, which is the kingdom of England. ...

Still, to reassure Parliament, she confirmed that she would not exclude the idea of marriage. But she felt strongly that it would be better for the country to choose a successor based an ability rather than bloodline—even descendants of highly capable rulers often proved to be degenerate. Her contemporaries provided excellent examples in support of her argument: Joanna, the sole heir to the crown of Spain, almost destroyed Isabella's great achievements because of her insanity. Don Carlos, son of Philip II of Spain and stepson of Mary Tudor, was born both physically and mentally deformed.

Parliament neither understood nor accepted Elizabeth's reasoning and kept pushing the issue of marriage. To quell the concerns, Elizabeth over time changed her wording from a flat "no" to "I hear you, and I'll think about it." When this ruse was exhausted, after 8 years on the job, Elizabeth switched tactics and decided to play along: She professed her willingness to marry and have children and accepted several successive suitors.

While Elizabeth was loath to share her wealth and power with any husband, marrying a foreign monarch would have been particularly portentous (even if the question of what role such a husband would play in England could have been resolved)—just look at Mary Tudor's marriage to Philip of Spain, which had resulted in war. A conjugal alliance with Scotland, on the other hand, might have been a terrific idea since it was a neighboring country with good merger potential, but Scotland was ruled by Mary, Queen of Scots, and later by her son, the boy-king James—neither of whom were marriage candidates.

To top things off, Elizabeth refused to name a successor. She had seen, under the reign of Mary Tudor how factions intent on overthrowing the ruling monarch tried to recruit successors to their cause, and she pointed to similar events in other kingdoms. Over time, as potential claimants died, James of Scotland emerged as the most likely successor. Implicitly, Elizabeth seemed to agree with his candidacy, and he did take the crown when she died. Alas, he turned out not to be the best possible choice. James was generally perceived as an ineffective ruler.

---

[1] Elizabeth, Speech 3. Repeated in Speech 4 to the Scottish Ambassador in 1561 later and in Speech 6 to Parliament in 1563.

4.2.3 From Loss to Profit

When Elizabeth rose to the throne, England was in dire straits both economically and politically. In 1560, Elizabeth instituted an important measure of currency revaluation and successfully averted hyperinflation: All coins were exchanged for new ones so that their nominal values were once again equal to their values in silver. The measure boosted trade as foreign merchants, who had refused to accept the old coinage, welcomed the new money.

Elizabeth stimulated trade and was a keen investor herself, supplying money and ships for the piracy expeditions of Sir Francis Drake and other voyages of exploration. Drake circumnavigated the globe from 1577 to 1580 with Elizabeth's financing and returned laden with Spanish booty. The Queen was quite happy and granted him a personal audience and a knighthood. Also funded by Elizabeth, Sir Walter Raleigh founded the first English colony (which he named Virginia, in honor of the Virgin Queen) in the Americas and was knighted upon his return. Elizabeth financially backed Admiral John Hawkins, the first British slave trader. In fact, largely because of Elizabeth's support, the slave trade became an important cash cow of the British Empire. Oddly enough, however, Elizabeth did nothing to exploit these opportunities for economic growth. Although England's economy had improved, its position relative to its competitors remained unchanged.

4.2.4 Dealing with the Competition

Elizabeth's predecessors had actively sought to conquer lands in Europe with the hope of enlarging England's holdings. Elizabeth, however, only engaged in battle to prevent the establishment of a united continent against England.[2] Thus Elizabeth supported French Protestants against their king, who was an ally of Spain, as well as the Dutch Protestants struggling to break free from Catholic Spain. She merely wanted to exert pressure on Spain and rapidly return to peaceful relations. England's military operations brought mixed results. Military strength was not enough to prevent the Spanish Armada from sailing to England in 1588, but it was enough to soundly defeat the Armada. That event, once again, offered a strategic opportunity to press forward to a decisive victory, which would have propelled England to become a major force in Europe. But Elizabeth declined to exploit it. Elizabeth was wary of big, lengthy military operations. She preferred to inflict economic, rather than military, damage, and once the immediate danger was past, the Queen was quick to reduce military expenditure (Fig. 4.3).

---

[2] This would become Britain's European strategy until the end of World War II.

Fig. 4.3 Map of Elizabeth' realm and the route of the Spanish Armada (© National Maritime Museum, Greenwich, London)

4.2.5   Renewing the Organizational Culture

Elizabeth did her best to become queen of the English rather than queen of the Protestants. The religious divide was deep when Elizabeth inherited the crown. To create a unifying value system, she decided to restore the Church of England, treading carefully to avoid offending Catholics too much.

Elizabeth was more tolerant of differing religious beliefs than many of her contemporaries: *In the sacrament of the altar, some think [one] thing, some [an] other; whose judgement is best God knows.*[3] She believed that the Church of England should be an independent institution governed by the monarch, and she wanted to retain many Catholic elements. So while she was prepared to reestablish a state religion, she would not go so far as to allow an inquisition. In 1559, Parliament named her the Supreme Governor of the Church. Elizabeth prevented the use of harsh measures to effect the transition. She did not want a recurrence of the persecutions that took place during Bloody Mary's reign.

Religious strife was far from over, however. In 1570, Pope Pius V issued a papal bull excommunicating Elizabeth. The pronouncement meant that as far as the Vatican was concerned, Catholic subjects of Elizabeth were no longer obliged to accept her as queen. The Counter-Reformation, led by missionary priests and

---

[3] Axelrod 108–109.

Jesuits, took hold several years later. Consequently, Parliament in 1581 passed several measures designed to constrain the threat to the state religion and to Elizabeth's authority. Though the severity of those measures was reduced at the request of the Queen, many priests still faced imprisonment, torture, banishment, and even execution. In total, 183 Catholics were executed during the last 25 years of Elizabeth's reign. (Appalling, certainly, but nowhere near the magnitude of atrocity that Bloody Mary sanctioned: 280 religious victims in just 5 years.) Elizabeth always insisted that the executions were carried out for reasons of disloyalty to the state and the monarchy and were not based on religion. Eventually, Elizabeth did succeed in creating a new, unified organizational culture through the Church of England.

4.3   Key Leadership Competencies

4.3.1   Vision and Strategy Development

Elizabeth's vision for her organization was to bring political, military, economic, and cultural stability to England. She worked to achieve and maintain that stability throughout her tenure, and she expressed this vision of continuity through the motto on her coat of arms: *Semper eadem* ("Always the same").

Though her vision was not particularly compelling and mobilizing, Elizabeth did have a strategy for achieving it. In a speech to Parliament in 1593, responding to criticism about failing to strategically exploit the defeat of the Spanish Armada 5 years earlier, Elizabeth stated:

> *This kingdom hath had many noble and victorious princes. I will not compare with any of them in wisdom, fortitude, and other virtues; but in love, care, sincerity, and justice, I will compare with any prince that ever you had or ever shall have. It may be thought simplicity in me that all this time of my reign (I) have not sought to advance my territories and enlarge my dominions, for both opportunity hath served me to do it, and my strength was able to have done it. I acknowledge my womanhood and weakness in that respect, but it hath not been fear to obtain or doubt how to keep the things so obtained that hath witholden me from these attempts; only, my mind was never to invade my neighbors nor to usurp upon any, only contented to reign over my own and to rule as a just prince.*[4]

In short, "I could have done it, but I didn't want to." Fair enough. It may not have been the best possible strategy, but a clear strategy it was. She stuck to it consistently and was unwilling to deviate from it, opportunity or not.

Elizabeth realized that she lacked not only ambition but also the right talent pool to implement a more aggressive strategy. Sir Francis Drake may have been a spectacular daredevil, but he was not on a par with Admiral Nelson. And in the field, no commander had qualities anywhere near those of the Duke of Wellington, the victor of Waterloo. Furthermore, as Elizabeth said herself, her commanders

---

[4] Elizabeth, Speech 21.

tended *to be transported with an haviour of vainglory* once they went into action.[5] For example, Elizabeth in 1589 sent two of England's most experienced naval officers (Drake and Norris) to lead a combined land and sea strike against the Spanish fleet. But because they chose to ignore the instructions of the Queen, the operation turned out to be a costly failure. In fact, England's campaigns on sea and on land often did not achieve the intended results. Not only did Elizabeth's commanders think nothing of disregarding their Queen's orders once on the scene, but Elizabeth herself sabotaged the chances for success by often refusing to give her commanders all the resources they asked for and purposefully limiting the interventions in time and scope.

The other three queens in this book benefited from life partners with whom they could realize ambitious visions. For Elizabeth finding a life partner who ticked all the boxes proved too big a puzzle: of sufficiently noble stock, with military qualities, from a suitable country for England to partner with, not a threat to the Queen's power, and someone she could love.

4.3.2 Leveraging Difference

Elizabeth was the second woman to rule her country. Interestingly, she inherited the throne from England's first queen, her half-sister Mary Tudor, and during the reign of her cousin Mary Stuart, Queen of Scots.

How did the leadership of those queens affect the way people viewed Elizabeth as a woman leader? Some concluded that it was "monstrous" to have a woman on the throne. In 1558, Protestant Scottish reformer John Knox published a pamphlet to that effect, aimed particularly at Mary Tudor, who was Catholic. When Protestant Elizabeth came to the throne, however, he backtracked, saying that she was an exception to the rule since her mission was to restore Protestantism. Others thought that being a woman on the throne was a tall order. John Foxe, therefore, tried to help by publishing a treatise on lessons from past queens in 1563.

What about Elizabeth's own perception of female leadership in light of the reigns of both Mary Tudor and Mary Stuart? There is little evidence that Elizabeth compared herself to them, but she did say that her reluctance to name a successor stemmed from her experience as a princess under Mary Tudor's reign. Still, she must have tried to learn from those two queens. Neither one of them was particularly popular with her subjects or considered to be a successful leader, and Mary Stuart was a direct competitor for the English throne. And Elizabeth must have concluded that marrying either a foreign prince, as Mary Tudor did, or a local nobleman, as Mary Stuart did (twice), would not be a recipe for success. Furthermore, Mary Stuart's love affairs with "bad boys" and subsequent marriages, which

---

[5] Somerset 514. Leicester's over-enthusiasm about his command to lead a force to the Netherlands, made the Queen believe that he sought rather his *"own glory than her true service"*: Somerset 414.

cost her the throne, must have reinforced Elizabeth's conviction to stay single. Elizabeth observed the other two queens' actions and then did the opposite.

Clearly, Elizabeth was well aware of the challenge she encountered as a woman leader in a man's world. She looked to God for support and guidance, voicing her loneliness and vulnerability in a prayer that she wrote in 1563, after 5 years on the job:

> *[W]hen the most prudent of kings (. . .), Solomon, frankly confessed that he was not capable enough unless Thou would bring him power and help, how much less am I, Thy handmaid in my unwarlike sex and feminine nature, adequate to administer these Thy kingdoms of England and Ireland, and do govern an innumerable and warlike people, or able to bear the immense magnitude of such a burden, if Thou, Most merciful Father, would not provide for me freely and against the opinion of many men.*[6]

To meet the challenge of being different, Elizabeth consciously leveraged a whole suite of positive female archetypes to her advantage: mother, virgin, female warrior, seductive maiden. By switching among the archetypes and adapting them to her audience, she prevented herself from being stereotyped. And, as an avid student of classical literature, history and the Bible, Elizabeth certainly knew her archetypes.

Elizabeth wanted her subjects to like her, and she worked hard to please them. From the start of her reign, she leveraged the positive archetype of the mother to qualify her leadership as a loving figure of authority: She would care for the English people, her "children," as if they were her own. In her so-called Golden Speech, given 2 years before she died, she said, *you never had or shall have any (prince) that will be more careful and loving.*[7]

Elizabeth's actions demonstrated her maternal affection. She intervened when she heard that the English soldiers in the Netherlands, there to support the revolt of the Dutch Protestants against Spain, were underpaid because of corruption. She personally wrote letters of condolence to the parents of noblemen and military officers who had lost a child. She agreed to make peace with the Earl of Tyrone, the leader of the Irish rebellion, and grant him amnesty in order to prevent further bloodshed. And she visited her direct reports on their sick bed to show her sympathy.

Elizabeth consciously associated herself with the Virgin Mary, who was not worshipped in Protestant England but whose image as a positive female archetype protecting her people with divine assistance was nevertheless present in people's minds. She highlighted this connection with the symbols she chose to include in her portraits. And the fact that England's first American colony, Virginia, was named after the Queen, shows that her efforts were successful. What's more, she could support her use of the archetype of queen as mother with a key biblical text for Protestants: *Kings will be your foster fathers, and their queens your nursing*

---

[6] Elizabeth, Prayer 9.

[7] Elizabeth, Speech 23.

mothers.[8] Another reference she exploited was that of Deborah, the Biblical leader and "mother" of the House of Israel.

Elizabeth did not present herself as a man. In fact, she leveraged her femininity in both appearance and behavior. Her unmarried, virgin status made her also into a "maiden", available for marriage. Elizabeth put a lot of attention to her clothing to appear both regal and attractive. As such, she could also play on the theme of the fair maiden, who received protection and attention from her knights. In the Elizabethan times, chivalry was still in high regard and she encouraged chivalrous behavior by her noblemen. She also genuinely enjoyed flirting on the job. She used the archetype of the seductive maiden with her direct reports and to even greater effect in her foreign policy to feign alliances through marriage.

Elizabeth acknowledged the prevailing prejudice against women and presented herself as different types of archetypical women, depending on the audience and the situation. To Parliament she once observed that as a *woman wanting both wit and memory* she had better shut up. Then she did quite the contrary—and most eloquently.[9] She began a presentation before the faculty and students of Cambridge University by stating that female modesty should prohibit her from delivering a rude and uncultivated speech to such an audience of learned men. She then went on to impress them by delivering her speech in flawless Latin, earning cheers of *Vivat Regina*.[10] Most famously, she addressed her army with *I know I have the body of a weak and feeble woman, but I have the heart and stomach of a king*.[11] In fact, what Elizabeth really did in these examples was to use a most effective influencing technique. By mentioning the stereotype up front, she revealed the "elephant in the room," so no one had to spend any energy pretending it wasn't there and could instead fully concentrate on what she had to say.

Still, some people in her environment felt uncomfortable because she was a woman and worried about her abilities to lead. Elizabeth was not afraid to address those concerns by asserting her formal authority when the occasion called for it. In 1566, for example, Elizabeth clashed with Parliament over her reluctance to marry and name a successor. Parliament at the time was nervous about general public discontent and the lack of foreign allies. Elizabeth defiantly responded that no one would force her into anything: *And though I be a woman, I have as good a courage, answerable to my place, as ever my father had. I am your anointed Queen. I shall never be by violence constrained to do anything*.[12] In modern words, "I am the boss around here, in case you forgot." It was noted that this outburst effectively shut up the audience.

Incidentally, Elizabeth's reference to her father in that speech, as on other occasions, should not be interpreted as taking on a masculine role. She simply

---

[8] Isaiah 49:23; Hackett 4.

[9] Elizabeth, Speech 5.

[10] Elizabeth, Speech 7

[11] Elizabeth, Speech 19.

[12] Haig 25; Somerset 187 and 191.

associated herself with the parent who was a strong ruler, which happened to be her father.

Similarly, when Elizabeth dressed in breastplate armor to deliver her famous speech to the troops assembled at Tilbury to repel the expected Armada, she was not taking on a male role either. She wore men's clothing because she was there in her capacity as a general, and military attire for women did not exist. In fact, she often associated herself with female warriors, who had the same weaponry as men. When she rode through the squadrons of her army, one eyewitness described her as *armed Pallas*,[13] referring to the virginal Greek goddess Pallas Athena, who was often depicted with helmet, breastplate, and shield. This was Renaissance England, after all, and such figures from classical antiquity were widely known, appearing frequently in theatrical productions. (Persons who wanted to influence the Queen often did so by sponsoring staged public entertainments in which Elizabeth was portrayed as the wise Pallas and the graceful Venus). She was also described as an Amazon, another unmarried female warrior from antiquity. Elizabeth probably also wanted to associate herself with the Valkyrie, the virgin female warrior from the Germanic sagas and also part of English mythology. The homegrown Valkyrie might well have been the right nationalistic image for Elizabeth to don against the foreign invaders from Spain.

Sir James Melville, the Scots ambassador to Elizabeth's court, once remarked, *Your Majesty thinks if you were married you would be but Queen of England; and now you are both King and Queen.*[14] His observation shows that the traditional role of the king was based on male titleholders. As a queen, Elizabeth had to clarify in her communications that she held power equivalent to that of a king in her own right. That is what Elizabeth did when she reminded her audience that she was their *anointed* Queen: She did not rule in anyone's stead, such as a deceased husband or minor son. Hence Elizabeth also tended to refer to herself as "prince," in the term's basic meaning of "ruler" or "monarch." It was a more gender-neutral moniker than "king" and a useful shortcut that did away with the need to clarify what kind of queen she was.

An elegant integration of her roles is depicted in a 1569 painting by Joris Hoefnagel: Elizabeth in full regalia towers over three goddesses from classical antiquity. The orb she holds both symbolizes royal power and the prize accorded in the beauty contest that set off the Trojan War. The power and control expressed by her stature contrast with the chaotic composition of the three goddesses. Elizabeth is superior because she unifies and embodies the positive key qualities of all three goddesses: the authority and care of the motherly Juno (Hera), the bravery and wisdom of the virginal Pallas Athena (Minerva), the beauty and femininity of the seductive Venus (Aphrodite). The artist who painted the picture clearly "got it." Elizabeth liked it so much that she kept it on display as part of the royal collection (Fig. 4.4).

---

[13] Elizabeth, *Collected Works*, 325 n1; Somerset 464.

[14] Somerset 94.

Fig. 4.4 Queen Elizabeth I
and the three goddessess
(Royal Collection Trust/©
Her Majesty Queen Elizabeth
II 2013)

4.3.3   Communication

Elizabeth demonstrated her competency in communication and her awareness of
the importance of reputation management very early on. In 1549, at the age of 15,
unfounded rumors spread about her involvement in a planned coup d'état against
her younger half-brother, the boy-king Edward VI. Rather than await interrogation,
Elizabeth took the initiative and flatly denied the rumors. She followed up with a
letter to the government, in which she mentioned that she preferred the slanderers
not to be punished because it would reflect badly on her. She went on to suggest that
the government itself should repudiate the rumors with a proclamation and ended
the letter with *written in haste*.[15] Elizabeth's course of action could have come
straight from a communications manual: She offered a solution rather than demanding retribution; she let others (the government) defend her reputation; she
depersonalized the issue ("It is not about me but about the king"); and she left
herself some room for backpedaling in case her letter was ill-received—she could
claim that, in her "haste," she had used the wrong words. The approach worked.

Elizabeth's coronation procession in London was as spectacular as it was
triumphal. At strategic points along the route, theatrical productions were staged
with carefully chosen subjects, such as Deborah who had lead the People of Israel to
victory. Another depicted the virtues that Elizabeth espoused: faith, love of her
subjects, wisdom, and justice. (Note that two of Elizabeth's key archetypes—the
caring, just mother and Pallas Athena, goddess of wisdom—reflected these virtues).

Every summer, Elizabeth took her court on a *progress*, a 10-week road show in
part of the country. These trips helped her to stay in touch with her subjects and
gave her subjects a glimpse of both the splendor of the monarchy and the humanity
of the Queen. Dressing up for the occasion was something Elizabeth did with gusto.

---

[15] Elizabeth, Letters 13 and 15.

Every year she celebrated her accession to the throne with an elaborate procession through London. She was a charismatic leader who took pride in being loved by her people.

Elizabeth's Armada speech in Tilbury is a good example of her leadership communication.[16] She took care to make sure her speeches were tailored for her audience. The Queen addressed Parliament eloquently and at length, but in front of the soldiers at Tilbury, she spoke briefly and to the point. She started out with claiming that people were her biggest asset: *I have placed my chiefest strengths and safeguard in the loyal hearts and goodwill of my subjects.* She then proceeded with:

> *I am come amongst you (…) being resolved in the midst and heat of the battle, to live or die amongst you all, to lay down for my God, and for my kingdom, and for my people, my honour, and my blood, even in the dust. I know I have the body but of a weak and feeble woman, but I have the heart and stomach of a king, and of a King of England too, and think foul scorn that Parma or Spain, or any Prince of Europe should dare to invade the borders of my realm; to which, rather than any dishonour shall grow by me, I myself will take up arms, I myself will be your general, judge and rewarder of every one of your virtues in the field. I know already for your forwardness, you have deserved rewards and crowns: and we do assure you, in the word of a Prince, they shall be duly paid you.*

In addition to placing herself among her troops, she spoke to her personal motivation. She also let them know that she would dictate their course of action (as their general), evaluate their performance (as their judge), and compensate it accordingly (as their rewarder). She committed herself to giving them what was due. She concluded by confirming that Leicester, as their commander, had her full trust and authority. Finally, her martial appearance must have been quite a sight.

4.3.4   Team Leadership and Delegation

Straight from the beginning, Elizabeth announced, *I mean to direct all my actions by good advice and counsel.*[17] Elizabeth's senior leadership team, the Privy Council, was the executive arm of the monarchy. It dealt with all issues, from military to economic and from legal to religious.

Mary Tudor before her had ruled through a Privy Council of 44 men. Elizabeth thought this far too big a span of control. Quite pointedly, she remarked, *I consider a multitude doth make rather discord and confusion than good counsel.* So one of her first measures was to reduce the leadership team to 19 men and then, later, to 11. She made sure to retain some of Mary's councilors, either because of their abilities or because of their political influence: The ardent Catholics, for example, could bear witness to Elizabeth's desire for religious peace. And for those ousted from the

---

[16] Elizabeth, Speech 19.

[17] Elizabeth, Speech 1.

Council, she had kind words, noting that they were let go not because of their lack of ability but to keep the group at a manageable size.[18]

The Earl of Leicester, right up to his death, was clearly Elizabeth's favorite direct report. But she did not enjoy good relationships with everyone on the Privy Council. In 1569, after 11 years on the throne, Elizabeth faced a serious issue with one member of her leadership team. The Duke of Norfolk, the highest-ranking aristocrat after the Queen, began maneuvering to gain more influence on the team, and then set his sights on marrying Mary, Queen of Scots, to gain her throne. When Elizabeth got wind of Norfolk's plans, she made him promise to abandon them. His frustration, however, drove him perilously close to rebellion. Elizabeth eventually had him locked up in the Tower of London and later executed.

Elizabeth then went after Norfolk's peers, the earls from the north, who had supported him. Not wanting to share his fate, they ignored her summons to court and rallied against her. Elizabeth replied with her army. Though she ultimately emerged victorious, it was at heavy cost: Elizabeth ordered the execution of more than 500 sympathizers and had two of Norfolk's men tortured to extract details that they had refused to disclose under ordinary interrogation. Elizabeth found out what was brewing rather belatedly. Had she attended team meetings more frequently, she might have been able to nip the whole matter in the bud.

There were other rough patches between the Queen and her team. Unhappy with her councilors' advice concerning the Netherlands, for example, she simply banned any further discussion of the matter. And she was most distressed that she allowed her team to talk her into approving the execution of Mary Queen of Scots.

The Queen often isolated herself from her direct reports, but she nevertheless lead them effectively overall in matters of finance, trade, and internal operations. She was less effective in military matters.

4.3.5   Talent Management

Elizabeth was loyal and forgiving toward the people who worked for her, and she chose most of her direct reports well. She worked with Sir William Cecil, for example, from her youth until his death in 1598. Soon after her coronation, Elizabeth named him Principal Secretary of State, a position similar to prime minister, with broad authority and powers of negotiation both at home and abroad. The young queen was quite clear about why she had chosen him: She believed he was loyal to the state and incorruptible.

Another good choice was Sir Francis Walsingham, who served the Queen as a foreign envoy and spymaster. Walsingham set up the precursor of what is now known as Her Majesty's Secret Service. It proved to be pivotal in uncovering several plots against the Queen. Then there were the naval commanders, Drake, Hawkins, Norris, and Raleigh—all of whom were competent.

---

[18] Axelrod 123; Somerset 66–67.

Leicester and Essex, however, she chose just because she liked them. The Earl of Leicester, member of Elizabeth' leadership team and her platonic lover, turned out to be a particularly bad choice. He not only talked Elizabeth into sending troops to support the French Huguenots in 1562, but he also convinced her to allow his brother the Earl of Warwick, a quite average military commander, to lead the expedition, which ended in defeat. Leicester also favored intervening in the Netherlands, and had championed the cause for years. Finally won over (or worn out) by his enthusiasm, Elizabeth put him in command of the English expeditionary force to the Netherlands in 1585. It was a risky decision because Leicester had not seen military service for almost 20 years. He disregarded the Queen's clear instructions and the venture ended in failure. Elizabeth became extremely angry and hurt by Leicester's insubordination. She told him, in 1586, that she had not expected such behavior from someone sponsored and favored by herself. Henceforth, she said, he would disregard her orders at his *uttermost peril.*[19] This difference between expectation and reality confirms that her affection for him overruled any doubts about Leicester's leadership competencies when choosing him for the job.

Compared to Leicester, Elizabeth's behavior toward Essex is even more baffling, when it comes to picking the right person for the right job. Essex was a noble youth keen on a leadership career in the service of his country. Elizabeth found him most charming. During one of his first jobs as a military officer, he joined Drake and Norris in ignoring Elizabeth's instructions during the expedition against the Spanish fleet in 1589. Elizabeth forgave him quickly, however, calling his actions *a sally of youth,*[20] and the following year she granted him a monopoly of importing sweet wines, which was highly lucrative. Drake and Norris, on the contrary, were summoned to appear before Elizabeth's leadership team to explain their behavior in the 1589 expedition. For the next few years, Elizabeth did not assign any military responsibilities to Drake. Still, she was not completely blind to Essex's faults. Though she succumbed to his pleas and handed him command of the army she sent to France in 1590, she felt that Essex was too impetuous to be put in the lead, and she warned the French king, Henry IV, of Essex's reckless streak. When Essex accomplished little, the Queen ordered her Privy Council to send a letter to him with negative feedback. In 1596, the crown ordered a raid against Cadiz. While the expedition was triumphant, all the booty ended up in the pockets of the participants—including Essex—instead of in the Queen's. Elizabeth received Essex coolly upon his return and did not grant him one of the senior positions in the leadership team he had sought.

In 1597, another major naval operation was organized against the Spanish, this time with Essex as its commander. At this point, the Queen wrote to him: *Remember that who doth their best shall never receive the blame that accidents may bring,*

---

[19] Elizabeth, Letter 62.

[20] Somerset 483.

neither shall you find us so rigorous as judge as to verdict enterprises by events.[21] Standing by itself, such a leadership statement seems quite supportive. It can be read as encouraging risks for greater returns and as an assurance that mistakes are to be expected. However, in the context of his previous performance, Essex read it as a license to experiment with impunity—which is exactly what he did. Elizabeth wanted to knock the Spanish navy out of action. But if that was accomplished successfully, she was prepared to allow her navy to capture the Spanish treasure fleet due in from the West Indies. Essex completely disregarded the primary objective and immediately headed for the Azores to intercept the treasure fleet. The English navy missed the rendezvous and returned empty-handed. Elizabeth once more sent Essex a letter with clear feedback, but he failed to see what he had done wrong. He returned to another cool reception by his Queen, and he reacted with a public sulk. Eventually, Elizabeth softened and gave Essex another honorary title, but he still remained rather impertinent—at one point during a heated discussion in the leadership team he turned his back to the Queen and publicly disagreed with her in violent terms.

Then, in 1599, Ireland rose up in rebellion. Elizabeth wanted to send Lord Mountjoy with an army to quell the uprising, but Essex put himself forward, arguing that Mountjoy had too little experience. Against her own good judgment—she did express her doubts—Elizabeth gave Essex the job. Despite getting all the resources he needed, he ignored Elizabeth's instructions yet again and failed dismally. Elizabeth sent him more letters with negative feedback and repeated what she expected of him, but they were about as effective as all her previous letters had been. Only when Essex left his command without authorization and returned to England to visit the Queen unannounced did Elizabeth realize that his insubordination had to stop. She withdrew Essex's import monopoly, effectively taking away his livelihood. Essex staged a rebellion, was arrested, convicted, and beheaded. Elizabeth subsequently did send Mountjoy to Ireland. He proved to be an effective choice, and Elizabeth was pleased to reward him with positive feedback.

What does this say about Elizabeth's development of her staff? Where as she was good at providing timely feedback, she did not help her staff members to develop their competencies in other ways. Overall, her penchant for strong personal relationships with members of her staff made her too forgiving of their lack of competence (Fig. 4.5).

4.3.6 Giving and Receiving Feedback

Elizabeth's feedback was of good quality. Elizabeth gave Drake and Norris negative feedback in 1589 about their divergence from the agreed objectives and the resulting underperformance in damaging the Spanish fleet. She explained what

---

[21] Elizabeth, Letters 95.

Fig. 4.5 Portrait of Robert Devereux, Earl of Essex (Metropolitan Museum of Art, New York) (http://commons. wikimedia.org/wiki/File:Robert_Devereux_Earl_of_Essex_ 22_Hilliard.jpg)

effect their actions had, not forgetting to include the impact on her own feelings.[22] She also showed personal affection. However, when she was angry she was not always able to channel her emotions constructively. She was known to have slapped one team member in the face and thrown a slipper at another.

Elizabeth tailored her feedback to the situation at hand. For example, she let Leicester know that failing to inform her that he intended to go against her instructions was worse than actually doing so and that she deplored his lack of progress reports. And when she wrote to Essex in 1599, she told him that she would have been less critical if he had shown some self-awareness about his failures.

Elizabeth was equally forthcoming with positive feedback, which was also of good quality. In a letter to Lord Hunsdon, Elizabeth expressed her thanks for his military success against the Northern Rebellion in 1570. She explained the impact of his performance and what it meant to her personally, and she announced that she would reward him financially. She wrote a similar letter to Lord Mountjoy for his success in Ireland in 1600. Her ability to give positive feedback and to do so generously certainly contributed to the motivation and loyalty of her staff.

She showed empathy in recognizing how her feedback was received by the people she normally favored. She also reset expectations after her feedback. She told her direct reports: *[W]ithout respect of my private will you will give me that counsel you think best, and if you shall know anything necessary to be declared of me of secrecy, you shall show it to myself only.*[23] Her council members felt that it was their duty to share differences of opinion with the Queen as long as they ultimately supported her final decision.

---

[22] For example Elizabeth, Letter 61 (her honor being touched by Leicester's disavowal of her instructions in the Netherlands).

[23] Elizabeth, Speech 1.

4.3.7 Performance Management

What was missing from Elizabeth's leadership style was consistency in follow-through. There were too few sanctions for bad performance and too many opportunities to try again. Two months after having given Leicester feedback in no uncertain terms about his insubordination in the Netherlands, Elizabeth wrote to him in a conciliatory and affectionate manner, thanking him for his efforts and letting him know that she still wanted to work with him. She recognized that he felt hurt by her feedback. She also asked him to understand why she felt hurt by his behavior. In any case, she did not want this event to lead to a breach between the two of them, and she was afraid to make matters worse by discouraging him. The letter for sure boosted Leicester's motivation, and in July 1586, Elizabeth tried to motivate him further. She showed empathy by telling him that he should not feel disheartened by the military successes of other English commanders.

However, when Elizabeth received a devastating evaluation of Leicester's performance from an emissary she had sent to assist him, she again lashed out against Leicester with strongly worded negative feedback. Leicester asked to be relieved of his command, which Elizabeth granted. When he returned to England, the Queen welcomed him warmly again. Two years later, in 1588, Elizabeth gave Leicester the command of England's army, assembled at Tilbury to withstand the Spanish invaders. Fortunately for England, the Armada never managed to disembark its troops.

Elizabeth led her direct reports at court better than she did those at a distance. She had trouble keeping military expeditions under control. At the beginning of her reign, her army in Scotland engaged the French contrary to Elizabeth's plan. Drake, Norris, and Essex disregarded her instructions concerning the Spanish fleet, and Leicester ignored her commands when in the Netherlands. The leaders of the raid against Cadiz in 1596 filled their own pockets with plunder instead of relinquishing it to the Queen.

Why did Elizabeth's commanders feel free to ignore her instructions? Did she lack credibility in military matters? Or did she give her staff ineffective incentives? It is true that Elizabeth's otherwise excellent education did not include military training and experience. The other queens in this book also lacked that competency and befriended men well versed in the art of war—Elizabeth chose to partner with amateurs.

More important was how Elizabeth managed motivation and incentives. She did not hit the right buttons with her direct reports. Honor on the battlefield was an important motivator for aristocrats of the Elizabethan era. So was financial gain through plunder. Yet Elizabeth tried to convey her own motivations that were based on efficiency to her staff: to protect and improve England's competitive position at the lowest possible cost. She also expected that personal relationships with her royal self would be highly motivating. Above all else, Elizabeth expected that her subjects would want to serve her. This is obvious in her positive evaluation of Lord

Mountjoy. She wrote that she was very happy that he was not driven by vanity or flattery but by a *true vow of duty and reverence of prince.*[24]

Interestingly, Elizabeth did not consider honor, pride, or solidarity as rewards. She did not use them in the Armada Speech at Tilbury. Yet the king in William Shakespeare's play *Henry V* addressed his troops on the eve of the battle of Agincourt with, *We few, we happy few, we band of brothers.* Shakespeare wrote *Henry V* in 1599, so the play is Elizabethan, and one might think that Shakespeare's speech would realistically reflect the times. Eyewitnesses state that Elizabeth did motivate her troops, but more simply by her presence than by her words. (Note the difference in approach between Elizabeth and Isabella in this regard: Elizabeth offered to pay her army what it was due, whereas Isabella promised her soldiers the opportunity to get rich.)

What is more, Elizabeth quickly built up a reputation of supporting military expeditions only reluctantly. She occasionally failed to give her commanders the resources they asked for, reneged on pay or resources that she had already promised, and did not always reimburse expenses. This led her staff to believe that they did not have their boss's full support, so they learned to look out for their own interests first. Thus a negative spiral was born: Elizabeth—with reason—did not fully trust the competencies of her commanders. Her commanders, for their part, not only felt that lack of trust but also felt—with reason—that their boss did not always set a course and follow it consistently. Each side second-guessed the other's motivations, which is not helpful, especially when leading from a distance. Elizabeth rarely was with her troops in person; her absence from the battlefield put her at a disadvantage.

4.4   Elizabeth' Leadership Impact

Elizabeth managed to transform England from a country torn with internal strife, threatened by foreign invaders, and struggling under a poor economy into a proud and stable nation with good economic prospects that could withstand competitive threats. The length of her reign was one of the key factors in this turnaround. She may not have won any wars, but she didn't lose any either. A more daring monarch would have leveraged growth opportunities in Europe and overseas, and England might have become one of the world's foremost powers more quickly. Still, Elizabeth left England with the elements that allowed for expansion in the seventeenth century: trade, naval power, good universities, a unified culture. Her hands-off approach toward Europe allowed the country to develop the unique, multifaceted insularity that would be key to its success for the next 400 years.

---

[24] Elizabeth, Letter 99.

4.5   What Women Can Learn from This Leader

Based on the discussion, above, we come to the following appraisals of her performance and leadership competencies.

Leadership Challenge	*Rating*
Career Direction	*Fully Achieved*
Dealing with the Competition	*Partly Achieved*
Regain Profitability	*Fully Achieved*
Succession Management	*Not Achieved*
Renewing Organizational Culture	*Fully Achieved*

Leadership Competency	*Rating*
Vision and Strategy Development	*Needs Development*
Leveraging Difference	*Strong*
Communication	*Strong*
Team Leadership and Delegation	*Competent*
Talent Management	*Competent*
Giving and Receiving Feedback	*Strong*
Performance Management	*Needs Development*

Elizabeth's pragmatic, economical approach and her refusal to be forced into action were beneficial for the turnaround that her organization needed. Rather than *semper eadem*, Elizabeth's motto could have been *in dubio, abstine* ("When in doubt, don't"). The recklessness of most of her military commanders probably only strengthened her in adhering to this motto of prudence. It applied also to her refusal to name a successor. She never developed an ambition to take her organization on a path of growth. However, once the turnaround was achieved, she could have found ways to strengthen her competitive position against Spain in particular. She lacked the military strength and talent for an all-out assault, but she could have been more active on the diplomatic front and constructed joint venture alliances against Spain. Without powerful foreign allies, England was forced into a protracted and exhausting war against Spain. Elizabeth equally lacked the vision to exploit the room for maneuver provided by the discoveries in North America. Alone at home and at work, Elizabeth lacked a strong partner to share her life and professional projects. It curbed her ambition and effectiveness. It might have benefited the country if, perhaps in 1588 after the Armada, Elizabeth had stepped down in favor of a leader with different qualities.

To Elizabeth, good leadership meant self-motivation, care, careful decision-making, a good team to spar with, and being married to the job. Her positive and negative feedback was timely, rich, factual, and to the point. Unfortunately, it was rendered ineffective by too much tolerance for underperformance by those whom she befriended. In the long run, providing stability for the country was no longer motivating. Without a glorious cause to serve, her staff sought individual glory. Whereas she selected some very talented people to work for her, at the same time and against better judgment she assigned jobs to incompetent people she personally liked. Since her leadership team's bench strength was fairly weak anyway, this had a negative impact on the overall results she achieved.

Much like the other queens in this book, Elizabeth had her dark side. Uprisings in England and Ireland were put down with severity. Mass executions, torture, violent executions, the slave trade—all were part of Elizabeth's toolbox.

Elizabeth's communication, in which she excelled, can be an example for modern women leaders. Her speeches were tailored for each type of audience. She put on an entertaining show and was able to reach all levels of society. She used all available means to get her message across, too—speeches, portraits, writings, theater, and personal appearance.

Elizabeth's strongest feature was her ability to turn her differences into opportunities. She fully leveraged the motherhood archetype to build her credibility as a woman leader. She wanted to lead as an archetypical mother might lead: with care, justice, defense rather than aggression, and economy. From the beginning to the end she pointed out how this distinguished her from both previous and future monarchs.[25] In 1587, at the height of the war with Spain, she defiantly stated that as a woman she was inclined to keep to peaceful relations. However, if someone dared to attack her she would be better at war than a man.[26] Nowadays, thanks to Sarah Palin, we would call this type of character a "Mama Grizzly."

Elizabeth amassed positive female archetypes: Virgin Mother, Pallas Athena, and Venus. She used such archetypes, unique to women and difficult to exploit by men, to great effect. She knew which archetype to use for which (male) audience. Modern women leaders can also be successful by distinguishing themselves from men rather than by imitating male behavior.

4.6 Top Five Do's and Don'ts from Elizabeth I

- Do
    - Select people in your team that can work together
    - Use a wide variety of communication tools
    - Take emotions into account when giving feedback
    - Be a leader to your entire workforce, despite diverging views
    - Turn your difference as a woman into an opportunity

---

[25] For example in her Golden Speech: *"care for my subjects"; "willingness to venture her life for your good and safety."* Elizabeth, Speech 23. Leicester and others described her as mother of her people.

[26] Levin, *Heart,* 140.

- Don't
  - Be too forgiving of underperformers
  - Stop being ambitious once you have achieved your goal
  - Overlook developing a successor
  - Expect people to be motivated by the same things as you
  - Underestimate the importance of powerful external allies

Bibliography

Axelrod, A. (2000). *Elizabeth I, CEO: Strategic lessons from the leader who built an empire.* New York: Prentice Hall Press.

Doran, S. (1995). Juno versus Diana: The treatment of Elizabeth I's marriage in plays and entertainments, 1561–1581. *The Historical Journal, 38*(2), 257–274.

Doran, S. (2003). Virginity, divinity and power: The portraits of Elizabeth I. In S. Doran & T. S. Freeman (Eds.), *The myth of Elizabeth* (pp. 171–199). Basingstoke: Palgrave Macmillan.

Fraser, A. (2002). *The warrior queens. Boadiccea's Chariot.* London: Phoenix Press.

Hackett, H. (1996). *Virgin mother, maiden queen: Elizabeth I and the Cult of the Virgin Mary.* Houndmills: MacMillan Press.

Haig, C. (1998). *Elizabeth I: Profiles in power.* Harlow: Pearson Education.

Levin, C. (1986). John Foxe and the responsibilities of queenship. In M. B. Rose (Ed.), *Women in the middle ages and the renaissance* (pp. 113–133). Syracuse: Syracuse University Press.

Levin, C. (1994). *"The Heart and Stomach of a King": Elizabeth I and the politics of sex and power.* Philadelphia: University of Pennsylvania Press.

Marcus, L. S. (1986). Shakespeare's comic heroines, Elizabeth I, and the political uses of androgyny. In M. B. Rose (Ed.), *Women in the middle ages and the renaissance* (pp. 133–135). Syracuse: Syracuse University Press.

Marcus, L. S., Mueller, J., & Rose, M. B. (Eds.). (2000). *Elizabeth I: Collected works.* Chicago: University of Chicago Press.

Somerset, A. (2003). *Elizabeth I.* New York: Anchor.

Taylor-Smither, L. J. (1984). Elizabeth I: A psychological profile. *The Sixteenth Century Journal, 15*(1), 47–72.

Catherine the Great: Leading Strategic Growth

Catherine the Great TIMETABLE

1729	Catherine born in Stettin, Northern Germany
1744	Travels to Russia to meet future husband Crown Prince Peter
1745	Marries Peter
1752	Starts love affair with Sergei Saltykov
1754	Birth of Paul, Catherine's first child and heir to the throne
1756	Starts love affair with Stanislas Poniatowski
1757	Birth of daughter Anna, who dies 2 years later
1758	Poniatowski sent back to Poland
1759	Starts love affair with Grigory Orlov
1761	Tsarina Elisabeth dies; Catherine's husband Peter becomes Tsar; Catherine now Tsarina consort
1762	April: Birth of Catherina's third child, Alexei, son of her lover Grigory Orlov. June: Catherine's coup d'état. September: Coronation to Catherine II, Empress of Russia
1763	End of the Seven Years War with Prussia. Russia victorious
1763	Catherina confiscates Church properties
1767	Catherine's river show on the Volga
1767–1768	Meetings of the Commission on the new laws, following Catherine's *Instruction*
1768	Catherine first to take the experimental inoculation against smallpox
1768–1774	First Russo-Turkish War
1772	First Partition of Poland. End of relationship with Grigory Orlov
1773–1774	Great Pugachev Rebellion against Catherine's rule
1774	Starts relationship and later marriages Grigory Potemkin. Potemkin named Governor-General of New Russia
1775	Provincial restructuring of Russia
1776	Love relationship with Potemkin ends
1776–1783	American War of Independence
1780	Catherine's trip to the new territories
1783	Annexation of the Crimean Peninsula
1785	Confirmation of the privileges of the aristocracy. Inspection tour of the improved canal system between the Volga and the Baltic Sea

(continued)

P. Vanderbroeck, *Leadership Strategies for Women*, Management for Professionals,
DOI 10.1007/978-3-642-39623-6_5, © Springer-Verlag Berlin Heidelberg 2014

1787	Catherine's road show through the newly acquired territories
1787–1791	Second Russo-Turkish War, ending in a Russian victory
1789	French Revolution topples the monarchy in France
1791	Death of Grigory Potemkin
1788–1790	Swedish-Russian War, after which both parties return to their original borders
1793	Second Partition of Poland
1795	Third Partition of Poland. Independent Poland ceases to exist until the end of Word War I
1796	Catherine dies at the age of 68

Catherine the Great—renowned for making Russia a world power in the late eighteenth century—is universally recognized for her legacy of territorial expansion, autocratic rule, and unconventional romance. However, this powerful czarina's leadership style and strategic genius were much more nuanced than this list, on its own, might suggest. She was a masterful and empathetic manager of talented people, a pioneer in using systems of merit-based performance rather than arbitrary patronage, and a skilled builder of internal and external networks—just to mention a few of her impressive managerial attributes. But before we explore precisely how Catherine the Great executed her unique brand of leadership and why her example should matter to today's women leaders, let's begin with some essential details about this fascinating leader's rise to power (Fig. 5.1).

5.1   Life and Career

Catherine II of Russia was born in 1729. Her parents ruled the tiny principality of Anhalt Zerbst, in Germany. At age 16, she married Grand Duke Peter of Russia, a grandson of Peter the Great who became Peter III in 1761, making her a czarina. (The author owes Catherine an apology: She appears in this book as one of four queens, but she was in fact an empress.) Six months later, Catherine staged a coup d'état and seized the throne; her husband was murdered shortly thereafter by Catherine's fellow conspirators. She never officially remarried, choosing instead to engage in a series of amorous relationships.

Catherine was a child of the Enlightenment. She read voraciously and corresponded with several French philosophers, including Diderot, Montesquieu, and Voltaire. Upon assuming the throne, she aimed first to clean up the prevailing economic mess and establish political stability—and then to modernize and aggrandize Russia. To a large extent, she was successful: She restructured Russia, reformed the legal and judiciary systems, set up education and health care systems, and liberalized the economy. She also modernized Russia's military forces to be on a par with those of other major European powers. Then, through a series of wars, she expanded Russia's borders to Prussia and the Black Sea. Catherine accomplished most of her goals through her long-lasting partnership—which was both professional and intimate—with Grigory Potemkin.

Fig. 5.1 Portrait of Catherine after her coup d'état (Erichsen, V. Equestrian Portrait of Catherine II. Oil on canvas. © The State Hermitage Museum, St. Petersburg/photo by V. Terebenin, L. Kheifets, Y. Molodkovets)

Despite her best efforts, however, Catherine was unable to modernize all levels of society. Her dependence on the support of the landowning aristocracy meant that large parts of the Russian population remained mired in the Middle Ages.

Catherine died of natural causes in 1796, at age 67, having reigned for 34 years. Her phenomenal rise from insignificant German princess to empress put Russia on the map as a force to be reckoned with, and it has remained a key actor on the world stage ever since.

5.2 Key Leadership Challenges

When Catherine became empress, she took on the following challenges:
- Directing her career
- Developing a vision and strategy for growth
- Leading a restructuring effort
- Creating a new organizational culture for Russia
- Ensuring her own succession

5.2.1 The Path to Power and Career Management

When Catherine married Grand Duke Peter, she moved from the obscure German principality where she had lived all her life to one of the most powerful courts of Europe. She decided to make the most of it, first by being a loyal wife to her husband and then, when that didn't work so well, by getting involved in politics at court.

Upon arriving in St. Petersburg, Catherine did her best to integrate quickly. She learned Russian and diligently followed the rituals of the Russian Orthodox Church. She also managed to get on her mother-in-law's, Czarina Elisabeth', good side. But her marriage was a disaster, and Catherine and her husband essentially lived independent lives. Catherine gave birth to her son, Paul, after 9 years and several miscarriages. Elisabeth took it upon herself to ensure the education of her grandson as the future czar; a practice not uncommon at the Russian court. Unfortunately for Catherine, the decision meant that she was seldom able to see her son.

Political tension ran high at the Russian court. Peter the Great had abolished male primogeniture as the method of royal succession. Instead, rulers could nominate any man or woman they chose, and a successor did not need to be a ruler's offspring. Ever since Peter the Great's death in 1725, therefore, competition was rife among factions and pretenders to the throne.

When Catherine's husband became czar in 1761, he quickly antagonized the aristocracy, the army, and the people by his leniency toward Russia's enemy, Prussia, and his disdain for Russian traditions and culture. Catherine, by contrast, began building relationships with senior civil servants and foreign ambassadors and immersed herself in court politics. The discontented at court converged around her, and Catherine began plotting a coup with coconspirators. Knowing that Peter's decision to withdraw from the war with Prussia dismayed Denmark and Austria, Catherine arranged secret loans from the two countries and then used the money to sway powerful fence sitters to her cause. Meanwhile, Catherine's lover at the time, Grigory Orlov, mobilized some 10,000 guards officers and troops with the help of his four brothers. Other regiments quickly joined the growing cause, and even the Church lent its support. Peter was stripped of his powers, briefly imprisoned, and subsequently murdered. In 1762, at age 33, Catherine became the empress of a country she had adopted a mere 14 years earlier.

Catherine's preparedness for the top job is evident in her personal notes from 1761, in which she sets out her leadership vision. She addresses the issue of serfdom, which she believed was both unjust and un-Christian. Realizing, however, that freeing the serfs would alienate the landowning aristocracy—upon whom she depended—she favored a gradual emancipation. To make better use of manpower and resources, Catherine also suggested moving manufacturing away from Moscow. Before issuing a new law, she aimed to encourage a broad-based discussion about it, as a law instituted out of the blue would not have the desired effects in society. She planned to give positive feedback, when earned, to her direct reports so that they would not be afraid to share their thoughts with her. She would select the right people for her team very carefully. That Catherine managed to realize most of this vision during her career attests to her diligence and discipline.

Coups and coup attempts happened time and again in Russia. Catherine herself had to fend off several threats to her own reign. The biggest challenge was Pugachev's Rebellion. Emelian Pugachev, a Cossack, started an insurrection in 1772 in the Ural region. His promises of land to the serfs and exemption from taxes increased his following among the oppressed. Because the Russian army was still occupied with fighting the Turks, the uprising provided a particularly dangerous threat to Catherine's power. With great effort and some good advice from Potemkin, Catherine quashed the revolt after 2 years.

Catherine sought legitimacy primarily through her deeds. She issued her first edicts on the very night of the coup and continued prolifically for the next 5 years in an effort to promulgate laws that would render the government more efficient. She also declared her son Paul to be her official heir, which her husband had failed to do. The move allowed her to claim that she governed on behalf of the infant, and since Paul was Peter the Great's great-grandson, the move lent an air of legitimacy to her reign.

Catherine stands out from the other queens in this book because of her love life. Whereas the others had few partners, Catherine had at least 12 official lovers, all considered handsome but some more professionally accomplished than others. Without exception, Catherine treated her paramours fairly, even the ones who betrayed her. After splitting up, she made sure that they kept the privileges she had awarded them and generously provided them with financial means for the future. Three lovers merit particular attention: Poniatowski, Orlov, and Potemkin.

Stanislaw Poniatowski was a striking, suave, sophisticated Polish aristocrat and diplomat who had distinguished himself as a military officer. He met Catherine in 1755, when he was 23 and she 26. He became her second lover during her unhappy marriage to Peter. Poniatowski was a central figure in Catherine's circle of friends in the years before she took power, when she was still developing her ideas about leadership. Their relationship lasted until 1758, when Czarina Elisabeth sent him back to Poland after she suspected Catherine of scheming behind her back. Catherine and Poniatowski had a daughter together, Anna, who died at age 2. Two years after Catherine was crowned czarina, she made Poniatowski the king of Poland.

Grigory Orlov was a Russian provincial nobleman, stationed in St. Petersburg as an officer in the Izmailovsky regiment of the imperial guards. Five years Catherine's junior, he was a handsome man of imposing physique with little formal education. He was known for his bravery in battle, in bear hunting, and as a boxer. His military experience and network in the army gave him a pivotal role in Catherine's coup d'état. Their relationship lasted more than a decade, from 1759 to 1772. They had one son, Alexey.

Catherine's first encounter with Grigory Potemkin was quite romantic: On the day of the coup in 1762, as Catherine led her troops in uniform, Potemkin, a petty guards officer at the time, noticed that her saber was missing its sword knot. He rode right up to her and offered her his own. Catherine took further notice of him when he later distinguished himself in the First Russo-Turkish War. A big man, Potemkin was well educated, cultured, and bright. At the same time he had a voracious appetite for wealth, power, food, and women. When their love affair began, Potemkin was 34 years old, and Catherine was 44. Right from the start, he became Catherine's principal adviser in political and military matters. He was also the chief architect and leader of Catherine's strategy for growing the Russian empire, and he shared her ideas for modernizing Russia. He was unquestionably the love of her life.

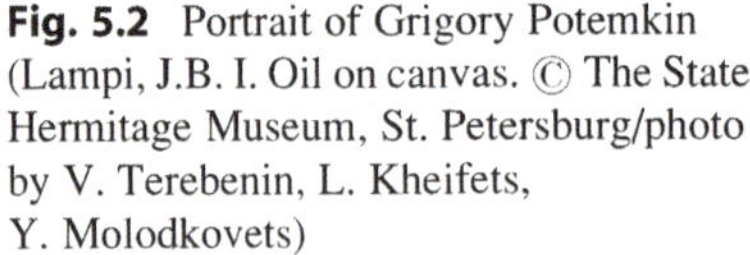

Fig. 5.2 Portrait of Grigory Potemkin (Lampi, J.B. I. Oil on canvas. © The State Hermitage Museum, St. Petersburg/photo by V. Terebenin, L. Kheifets, Y. Molodkovets)

Catherine and Potemkin married in secret in 1774. When their highly passionate relationship cooled after 2 years, Potemkin began to personally select most of Catherine's new lovers. He knew her taste in men, of course, but he also wanted to ensure that no one had the potential to become a rival for his professional partnership with her. Catherine and Potemkin's relationship lasted until he died, in 1791, at age 52 (Fig. 5.2).

Whereas Catherine's other lovers were mere companions and bedfellows, these three were vital in her professional life. Poniatowski was key to the development of Catherine's leadership ambition and philosophy. Orlov was indispensable for seizing and consolidating power. Potemkin was critical to the implementation of Catherine's vision and strategy of growth.

5.2.2 Developing a Vision and Strategy of Growth

Catherine annexed the Ukraine, the northern Black Sea coast, and the Crimea after two victorious wars against the Turks in the south. Apart from adding land, these acquisitions put an end to the constant raids from the Tatars. In the north, Catherine fended off an attack from Sweden. In the west, working with Prussia and Austria, Catherine helped carve up Poland and acquired modern-day Belarus. In the east, she favored the exploration and settlement of what is now Alaska. But her hope of reconquering Constantinople from the Turks and re-establishing the Byzantine Empire never came to fruition.

When Catherine took power, her country was in dire straits. Money was tight, management was poor, and corruption ran rampant. Her first measure was to cancel the war plans and alliances of her husband to reduce military expenditures. She then temporarily suspended corn exports to keep a check on the price of bread. Reducing expenses alone was not enough, however. Catherine needed to increase state income to finance her plans for reform.

Catherine grew the Russian economy in a dynamic way. She did so, first, by adding fertile land and stimulating agricultural production. Her conquests in the south, for example, not only provided arable territories but also allowed Russia to ship its corn surplus to western Europe via the Black Sea.

Second, Catherine obtained external financing. She was the first Russian leader to secure loans from banks in Amsterdam, then the world's financial center. She financed the first war against the Turks with such a loan and paid half of it back with the indemnity Russia had received from the defeated enemy. Her actions helped strengthen Russia's credit worthiness as well. The country advanced from a credit rating of B+ to A+ while the interest due dropped to 4 %. (France's credit, by comparison, was considered junk status and had to pay 12 % during the same period.) Catherine also found money through the Church. She continued her husband's initiatives to curtail the Church's financial wealth and diverted a large part of its income to her treasury.

Third, Catherine implemented a policy of market liberalization. Russia's traditional exports of wood, shipbuilding materials, iron, and precious metals increased thanks to her efforts, and foreign trade tripled. Russia also enjoyed a constant trade surplus. In 1766, the country signed a commercial treaty with Great Britain, agreeing to supply Russian commodities for the growing demand of British manufacturing industries. Catherine promoted entrepreneurship by discouraging state intervention, creating a state bank to provide long-term loans at advantageous interest rates, and introducing paper money (in 1768).

Later, as part of the organizational restructuring she began in 1775, Catherine introduced financial institutions, throughout the country, that provided better insight into the nation's finances. She also became the first czar to use a yearly budget. This reform, too, considerably increased Russia's credit rating in the financial markets.

One measure of Catherine's success was that the Russian population grew from fewer than 30 million people to 44 million during her reign. Half of that growth is attributable to territorial acquisitions, the other half to immigration and natural growth. Catherine actively invited immigrants to settle and develop the vast new lands of Russia. She provided an attractive package of benefits, such as interest-free loans and exemption from taxation and military service, to those who accepted her offer. Many German and French immigrants heeded her call. Potemkin oversaw the construction of new cities, such as Odessa and Dnepropetrovsk, and provided incentives for people from all over Russia to move to the south (Fig. 5.3).

Fig. 5.3 Map showing the territories acquired by Catherine (© The Florida Center for Instructional Technology, www.fcit.usf.edu)

5.2.3   Restructuring Russia

By the time Catherine took power, Russia had been experiencing instability in its leadership for almost 40 years. Catherine's mother-in-law, Elisabeth, ruled for two decades with neither vision nor strategy. Just as her predecessors had done since the death of Peter the Great, Elisabeth essentially left the task of government to her direct reports. Furthermore, contradictory and overlapping laws resulted in inefficient and ineffective processes. Catherine's immediate opportunity was to provide the stability the country craved, but her ambition went beyond that. To modernize and expand Russia as she wished, however, Catherine needed an organizational strategy that would provide the necessary resources to sustain growth.

Catherine's approach to government was more like that of her native country, Germany, and she spent an enormous amount of energy trying to make Russia's leadership more efficient. Catherine set out her principles of good governance and organization in a 500-page document called *Nakaz* (Great Instruction), which drew heavily on literature from the contemporary philosophers of the Enlightenment. In 1767, Catherine launched a major initiative to improve policies and procedures that she hoped would transform the organizational culture. She established a commission with members from all levels of society and tasked them with drafting proposals to revise Russian law using the principles in the *Nakaz*. The commission was dissolved, however, when the first Russo-Turkish war broke out in 1768 and most members had to take up military service.

Between 1775 and 1785, Catherine implemented a major organizational restructuring aimed at solidifying her authority, increasing efficiency, and implementing management standards throughout the empire. This project benefited greatly from the ideas and support of the legislative commission. The 25 provinces were sliced into 41, and each province was then subdivided into districts. Further decentralization was achieved by transferring some of the power from the provincial governors to newly created institutions: courts, police officers, and boards of education and welfare.

In practice, the reform was hampered by a lack of available and educated talent to fill the new positions. To counteract this problem, Catherine sponsored education. She ordered the establishment of free elementary and secondary schools for boys and girls in provincial towns, and, in 1764, she created the Smolny Institute for young girls of the aristocracy and the bourgeoisie. The school's purpose was to educate women who would then properly educate their children. Catherine also founded Moscow University and the Academy of Fine Arts. She reformed the curriculum of the school for military officers into a real school of public management, so that its graduates would also be suitable for leadership positions in the government.

To increase Russia's population, Catherine not only stimulated immigration but also invested in health care. She founded a medical college and financed the building of several hospitals that offered free medical care to the poor.

Catherine felt that she needed the support of members of the aristocracy more than they needed hers: After all, they had brought her to power and had helped her stay there. Thus, in 1785, Catherine confirmed and extended the privileges of the aristocracy. She decreed that persons of noble birth could be judged only by their peers and were fully entitled to the proceeds of their lands. The French Revolution in 1789 confirmed to Catherine that she had made the right decision.

For similar reasons, Catherine did nothing to eradicate serfdom throughout Russia. Under the archaic system, property holders owned not only land but also the peasants who worked it, essentially as slaves. Catherine left the system unchanged for three reasons: First, freeing the serfs would have deprived the aristocracy, upon whom she depended, of cheap labor. Second, Catherine's plans for expansion required a large army, and serfs were a convenient and abundant source of cannon fodder to fill the ranks. Third, Catherine's passion for liberal ideas had chilled somewhat after Pugachev's Rebellion.

5.2.4 Renewing the Organizational Culture of Russia

Catherine was successful in her efforts to effect change in management culture. After she abolished torture, carrying out justice had to depend on a culture of objectivity and factual analysis rather than forced confessions. Catherine also upgraded the skills of Russia's ruling class by introducing the Russian elite to western European culture and regularly inviting philosophers, artists, and economists of the Enlightenment to court in St. Petersburg. She established an objective method of performance management, replacing arbitrary hirings and firings with meritorious evaluation.

The overall culture of Russia, however, remained authoritarian, which stifled innovation and renewal. The combination of an economy largely based on the production of commodities, Catherine's disinclination for sharing power, and her reluctance to abolish serfdom prevented true modernization.

5.2.5 Ensuring Her Own Succession

Catherine had an ambiguous relationship with her son and heir, Paul. She nominated him as her successor, but little love was lost between mother and son. When he married and produced an heir, Catherine—just as her mother-in-law had done with Paul—she took her grandson, Alexander, away from his parents to oversee his education herself. She was a fan of Jean-Jacques Rousseau and applied novel ideas to Alexander's upbringing.

Catherine clearly enjoyed her role as grandmother and had a far better relationship with her grandson than with Paul. Indeed, it seemed that she was oblivious to the emotional damage she had inflicted on her son by allowing Elisabeth to take him away, by killing his father, by taking Paul's children away from him, by regarding him as a rival and keeping him away from government affairs, and by her affection for her grandson. Perhaps unsurprisingly, when Paul succeeded his mother in 1796, he spent more time undoing her legacy than he spent governing his empire. A case in point was that he promulgated a law to exclude women from ascending to the throne. Overall Paul was regarded an ineffective czar.

5.3 Key Leadership Competencies

5.3.1 Vision and Strategy Development

Catherine ran her government much more smoothly than her predecessors had done, in large part because of her willingness to consult advisers and stakeholders before taking action. For the most important reforms, she put working groups in place, and she always used facts to inform her decisions. She said:

One learns more talking to ignorant people about their own affairs, than in addressing oneself to the experts, who have nothing but theories, and who would be ashamed not to reply with ridiculous assertions on things about which they have no real knowledge. (These experts) they never dare pronounce these four words: "I do not know", which are so useful to the rest of us ignorant people, and which sometimes prevent us from making dangerous decisions; for, if in doubt, it's better to do nothing than to do the wrong thing.[1]

Catherine also managed stakeholders deftly. By allowing committees to discuss her plans in advance, she secured buy-in. She kept peaceful relationships with Prussia and Austria so that she could concentrate on southern expansion (the Second Russo-Turkish War was actually a joint venture with Austria). Her timing of the annexation of the Crimean peninsula was brilliant: Britain and France, who frowned upon Russia's growing power, were still mired in the U.S. War of Independence.

Catherine sometimes took modest risks to avert bigger ones. For example, when the British wanted to cut off trade to starve the American revolutionaries, she brought several countries together in "armed neutrality" to ensure continuity in overseas commerce.

Catherine saw the potential of Russia as a sleeping giant and set out to wake it, building on the foundational work of Peter the Great. In implementing her strategy, she considered all angles—financial, technical, and personnel-related. She targeted both organizational structures and infrastructure. And she marketed her ideas—and herself—adeptly.

5.3.2 Building and Maintaining a Network

Before seizing power, separated from her husband in all but name, Catherine built a network in the imperial court. Finding both love and a purpose outside her marriage, she became embroiled with the various competing factions at court. She debated what to do once her husband, whom she and some of her confidants considered incompetent, became czar. She sought out senior mentors such as Sir Charles Hanbury-Williams, an experienced diplomat and British ambassador. Networking with people like Panin and the Orlov brothers allowed Catherine to seize power, and her strong relationship with the aristocracy helped her to keep it.

---

[1] Dixon, *Catherine* 2009, 283; Rounding 428.

Catherine also networked with ambassadors of important foreign powers and made use of informants. This system needed greasing with presents, and Catherine was constantly short of money. When she accepted financial support from the British government, who saw in her a worthwhile investment, she made clear that she was taking the money for Russia, not for herself.

Catherine made a conscious effort to get in the good graces of potential enemies. Looking back on this episode of her life, she wrote:

> *I tried to be as charming as possible to everyone and studied every opportunity to win the affection of those whom I suspected of being in the slightest degree ill-disposed towards me; I showed no preference for any side, never interfered in anything, always looked serene and displayed much attentiveness, affability, and politeness all round.*[2]

Without any doubt Catherine already before assuming power used networking effectively to build and protect her reputation at home and abroad.

5.3.3 Talent Management

Catherine filled the talent pipeline by investing in the leadership education of promising prospects, and then she actively managed that talent. The czarina shared her wisdom with her grandson, the future Czar Alexander I: *Tolerate an unpleasant person in your sight, and do not glance askance at him: a man who can get on only with people he likes, and not with those he does not, is lacking in wisdom.*[3] During her first year in office, Catherine looked keenly for the best talent and started making appointments, rewarding the people who had helped her stage the coup.

She commissioned her lover Grigory Orlov with overseeing the settlement of German immigrants in the empty lands of southern Russia—a brand-new post to which no one else could lay claim. Grigory's brother Alexei, nominated admiral by Catherine, would distinguish himself in the First Russo-Turkish War.

Count Nikita Panin, who had actively supported Catherine's coup, became Minister of Foreign Affairs at age 44. One of Catherine's most trusted advisers, he would remain in this position for the first half of Catherine's reign. Catherine cherished Panin's experience and advice, although their opinions on matters of governance differed greatly. Panin favored a strong management team with delegated powers, whereas Catherine preferred not to delegate to anyone but Potemkin. Catherine also appreciated that Panin was incorruptible.

Prince Alexander Vyazemsky, Procurator-General and Finance Minister for most of Catherine's reign, had the idea to introduce paper money. He presided over the newly decentralized financial offices, substantially increasing the government's tax intake. From abroad Catherine recruited John Paul Jones, who

---

[2] Rounding 48.

[3] Dixon, *Catherine* 2009, 134.

had a good track record as a navy admiral in the U.S. War of Independence, although he failed to repeat his successes in the service of Russia.

Potemkin, 10 years Catherine's junior, became her chief operating officer and eventually the number-two leader of Russia. Catherine put him in charge of Russia's military forces and, given his achievements, promoted him several times. Later he became both the architect and the builder of New Russia, her huge conquests to the south. Catherine recognized Potemkin's potential and empowered him to realize her vision of a greater Russia. He won the Second Russo-Turkish War.

Potemkin was also Catherine's partner in matters of communication. During the grand tour of New Russia in 1786, he staged parties, displays, and visits to impress Catherine's foreign entourage. This inspired the legend of the *Potemkin Villages*: mere façades put along the road to give a false impression of growth and progress. This legend, fabricated by people jealous of Catherine, is an insult to both Catherine's sense of rigor and Potemkin's capacity to deliver. It amounts to nothing more than when local managers give their site an extra sweep before the CEO visits. Catherine particularly appreciated Potemkin's intelligence, his competence as a military leader, and his ability to spar with her over strategy. She was devastated for months after he died.

Catherine did not hesitate to replace people who failed to meet her objectives. When the first attempts to quell the Pugachev Rebellion failed, she put a new general, Bibikov, in charge of military operations and of identifying the causes of the rebellion. Catherine also replaced Panin as foreign minister when his opinion diverged too far from hers.

When Potemkin died, Catherine had trouble replacing him. Platon Zubov, Catherine's 24-year-old lover who was neither experienced nor particularly competent, was quick to fill the vacuum and seize influence at court. Fortunately for Catherine, no real challenges emerged during the final 5 years of her reign.

5.3.4 Performance Management

Catherine was a hard-driving manager known for giving positive feedback in public and negative feedback in private. She incited her subordinates to work harder and did not spare criticism when deliverables were late. She even rebuked two French diplomats who made rude remarks about Muslim women over dinner, telling the Frenchmen that the people of Russia were to be respected in their diversity. She also pressed Potemkin for results when his conquests of cities and forts were not forthcoming.

Nevertheless, Catherine was willing to give people a second chance. For instance, she refused the resignation of Admiral Nassau-Siegen after his errors led to the loss of a battle against the Swedes, because his prior track record had been good. She also successfully re-motivated a despondent Potemkin several times— for example, after the initial stages of the war against the Turks.

Catherine shared her ambition with her direct reports for inspiration. To one of her field marshals she said: *I wish our nation to shine in all the military and civil virtues and that we should surpass all other nations in every genre.*[4] She consistently showed clear appreciation for Potemkin's achievements and asked him to nominate members of his staff for promotion on the basis of merit.[5] To Panin, her foreign minister, who had been instrumental in getting Poniatowski on the Polish throne, she wrote: *Nikita Ivanovich! (...) This event greatly increases my trust on you, since I see how faultless all your measures were. I didn't want to miss showing you how pleased I am.*[6]

Potemkin was a prima donna, prone to sulking after a setback. In 1787, when the Russian fleet was damaged in a storm on its way to attack the Turks in the Black Sea, Potemkin wanted to relinquish his command. Catherine told him not to behave like a 5-year-old,[7] and he begrudgingly went back to work. A month later, when he found fault with Catherine's handling of the Austrian alliance in the war against the Turks, he took her negative reaction personally, cutting off communication with her for a month. Later, after reminding Catherine how much he had done for her, Potemkin said, *If I am out of place, then, of course, in the future I'll speak only on those matters that have been entrusted to me.*[8] Their relationship returned to normal.

We get another glimpse of Catherine's preferred leadership style in a letter she wrote in 1763 to Vyazemsky as Procurator-General:

> *If I see that you are loyal, hard working, open and sincere, then you can be assured of my unbounded confidence. Above all I love the truth, and you must feel free to say it, without fear; you can argue with me without danger, provided that the end result is good.*[9]

Catherine deeply appreciated honest advice but within limits. Alexander Radishev, a Russian intellectual, published a book in 1790 (a year after the French Revolution) about the abuses of serfs that he had witnessed on his voyage from St. Petersburg to Moscow. Catherine, scared by the events in France, had the book banned and sent Radishev to Siberia.

To make Russia's workforce more effective, Catherine introduced a fixed-salary and pension scheme for civil servants and teachers, so that they depended more on the state than on bribes. She also implemented systems of inspection and performance appraisal. Still, ending corruption and instituting meritorious promotion proved to be difficult.

---

[4] Dixon, *Catherine* 2009, 204.

[5] Smith 144 (Catherine to Potemkin 20/07/1783), 145 (Catherine to Potemkin 26/07/1783), 150 (Catherine to Potemkin 13/08/1783).

[6] Dixon, *Catherine* 2009, 186.

[7] Smith 205 (Catherine to Potemkin 02/10/1787).

[8] Smith 213 (Catherine to Potemkin 23/11/1787) and 215 (Potemkin to Catherine 25/12/1787) and 334 (Catherine to Potemkin 30/12/1787).

[9] Dixon, *Catherine* 2009, 134; Rounding 177–178.

5.3.5 Delegation

Catherine believed in absolute rule. She delegated certain tasks and institutions to individual direct reports, but she never constituted an elite management team that would meet to aid her in leadership decisions. Her preferred method was to develop an idea on her own and then discuss it with one or more direct reports or let an ad-hoc committee consider it, before taking the final decision herself. For example, with her deputy, Potemkin, she discussed key decisions on staffing, taxation, foreign affairs, and how to deal with Pugachev after his capture.[10] She did sometimes set up a project team, such as for the war against Turkey.

Catherine was probably unaware that the combination of her work ethic and absolute authority fostered what she sometimes considered her subordinates' irksome dependence. In 1771, then 9 years in office, she wrote this about a matter that was referred upward to her for resolution:

And so, having wasted an entire morning, every minute of which is valuable to me, on an affair that could have been resolved according to the laws without me, I now send it back so that the Senate can finalize it accordingly.[11]

Catherine's perfectionism undoubtedly contributed to this phenomenon. For example, she required that every piece of correspondence to ambassadors or foreign governments be presented to her in full, not merely in summary, for approval. Looking back on her career, she attributed any failures to the fact that *things were not carried out with the exactitude that I prescribed.*[12]

What worked out well was delegating the southern half of Russia and all military matters to Potemkin. She gave him money and other resources for his campaigns of conquest. Catherine depended a lot on Potemkin, but she also allowed herself to eschew his advice. For example, in matters concerning Prussia, she felt more qualified than he, as she had spent her youth there.

Catherine's leadership style prevented her from leaving a management structure that could ensure continuity under a less capable or less mature leader. More important, it prevented her from fostering teamwork among her senior management. Because both she and Potemkin were such strong leaders and hard workers, she never saw anyone else as measuring up, and she therefore never built a strong leadership bench. This became apparent after Potemkin died, when rivalries among senior managers sprang up. Catherine, in her sixties, struggling with her health and distraught by Potemkin's passing, could not wield the strong leadership she once had.

What's more, given her northern German Protestant work ethic, Catherine was impatient and constantly reminded people not to waste time. Her emblem as she

---

[10] Smith 41 (Catherine to Potemkin 29/07/1774), 48 (Catherine to Potemkin December 1774), 58 (Catherine to Potemkin March 1775), 110 (Catherine to Potemkin 23/05/1780).

[11] Dixon, *Catherine* 2001, 143.

[12] Dixon, *Catherine* 2001, 143.

wrote to French philosopher Voltaire, was *a bee, which flying from plant to plant, collects honey to carry to its hive, and its inscription is utility.*[13] A bee, it should be noted, works hard and does not delegate.

Catherine kept grueling hours throughout her reign. She got up at five or six in the morning to read and write for about 4 hours. Then she started her business meetings. She often would not stop working until at 10 o'clock at night, 6 days a week. Catherine's amorous affairs were her only outlet in a life otherwise filled with discipline, hard work, and little indulgence in food or drink. She increased her personal productivity by employing three state secretaries. Overall, Catherine's capacity to delegate could be vastly improved. She epitomized the mantra "If you want it done right, do it yourself."

5.3.6 Leveraging Difference

Catherine, in effect, succeeded her predecessor Elisabeth, as Catherine's husband's reign was extremely short. Elisabeth's main positive feature was that her reign was uninterrupted. The Russian army, modernized by Peter the Great, did well in the Seven Years' War from 1756 to 1763, but otherwise Russia was led at that time by Elisabeth's favorites at court, not by Elisabeth herself. Catherine, installed by her lover, a guards officer, was expected to follow suit. Some of Catherine's wayfarers, such as Count Panin, later Catherine's Foreign Minister, expected her to rule only on behalf of her underage son.

Catherine's behavior was scrutinized in light of her gender, sometimes with approval and sometimes not. The primary issue was not that she had sexual relationships out of wedlock, but rather that she gave relationships with her lovers an official status. Catherine herself confessed to Potemkin, *Had fate given me in my youth a husband whom I could've loved, I would've remained true to him forever. The trouble is that my heart is loath to be without love even for a single hour.*[14] Her behavior made it easy for her critics to use stereotypes of the weak, irrational, wanton woman against her, and her sex life was mocked in cartoons. Nevertheless, she earned respect for her achievements in office.

Catherine also had a female contemporary in Maria Theresia of Austria, but Catherine seems not to have paid attention to her, as either a role model or an anti–role model. Catherine immediately made clear, though, that her reign would differ from Elisabeth's. She staged an awesome coronation only a few months after seizing power and quickly issued a flurry of new laws. In her first 2 years, she arrested, tortured, executed, or banned to Siberia dissident military officers whom she suspected of planning a countercoup. She also broke with the tradition of firing her predecessor's staff. If they performed well, they could continue their careers under her. Catherine used her authority and fairness to run a tight ship and, unlike Elisabeth, did not allow her direct reports to undermine her.

---

[13] Rounding 199.

[14] Smith 10 (Catherine to Potemkin 21/02/1774).

Fig. 5.4 Catherine as Athena on her coronation medallion (National Museum of Finland) (http://commons.wikimedia.org/wiki/File:Accession_of_Catherine_II,_1762,_Russia,_by_J._G._Waechter_-_National_Museum_of_Finland_-_DSC04120.JPG)

Catherine carefully managed her public image, consistently presenting herself as a modern-day Pallas Athena (Minerva), the armed goddess of wisdom. Indeed, on her coronation medallion, Catherine was shown wearing a breastplate and helmet, and she cast herself in the role of the goddess at various public events. A statue erected in her honor in Potemkin's palace in 1789 also depicted Catherine as ruling by the strength of her wisdom (Fig. 5.4).

Pallas Athena was also unmarried, and given that Catherine's marriage to Potemkin was never made public, she thereby completed the parallel with the goddess and turned a potential source of criticism into an advantage. Catherine assumed a role as the stern school teacher of the nation, bringing the leadership practices and values of modern Europe to backward Russia. As an Athena, she could be the defender of the realm without apologizing for her gender.

Immediately after the coup, Catherine commissioned a portrait in which she is shown on a horse, sword in hand, dressed in a guards officer's uniform to honor the guards whose support helped her seize power (Fig. 5.1). Later, to celebrate military victories, she showed herself again in an army or navy uniform, not to be an imitator of men but to honor the men she led.

Catherine did not completely break with precedent. Czars and czarinas were traditionally addressed as "*batyuska*" ("little father") and "*matushka*" ("little mother"), respectively. Potemkin and the Orlov brothers, frequently addressed her in this way.[15] Potemkin erected a statue for her in his palace in St. Petersburg, inscribed *To the Mother of the Fatherland*.[16] In 1767, when Catherine issued the *Nakaz*, the committee members were so impressed by the document that they offered to bestow her with the titles The Great, The Wise, and Mother of the Fatherland. Catherine modestly refused the titles, except for Mother. She happily embraced the association in Russian literature between female monarchs and the Virgin Mary, who leads her people to happiness. Catherine played the role of mother by, for example, writing letters of consolation to direct reports when their significant others fell ill. Her investments in health care and education reinforced

---

[15] For example Smith 255 (Potemkin to Catherine 18/07/1788) and 382 (Potemkin to Catherine 29/04/1791); Dixon *Catherine* 2009.

[16] Smith 371.

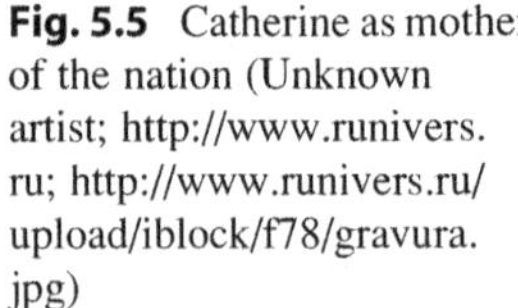

Fig. 5.5 Catherine as mother of the nation (Unknown artist; http://www.runivers.ru; http://www.runivers.ru/upload/iblock/f78/gravura.jpg)

the image of Mother of the Fatherland. An engraving shows Catherine in 1782 surrounded by family and senior executives such as Potemkin and Panin (Fig. 5.5). The caption is written in Latin, which indicates that the message is addressed at the management population. It translates as *Oh, you very fortunate subjects! As she loves her children, so she loves you.*

In individual interactions, too, Catherine leveraged her difference. To motivate Potemkin she used a male archetype for him and a female archetype for herself. In their correspondence, the two played with the metaphor of Potemkin in the role of the valiant knight who courts the favor of his queen by heroic deeds,[17] a Russian variation on Sir Lancelot and Queen Guinevere.

Both in interactions with groups and with individuals Catherine consciously leveraged several positive female archetypes to her advantage: armed goddess of wisdom, schoolteacher, mother, and legendary queen. By switching between them and adapting them to the audience, she prevented herself from being stereotyped.[18]

5.3.7 Communication

Just as Cleopatra went on a tour of the Nile, Catherine travelled down the Volga and the Dnepr. She took foreign diplomats with her in the guise of "embedded journalists". In her first 5 years in power, Catherine made extended trips to three different parts of her territory. In 1780, she toured the country to assess how her provincial reforms were working and to visit the newly conquered lands. In 1786, she went to inspect the canal improvements between the Volga and St. Petersburg. In 1787, for her 25th jubilee as empress, she travelled to the new territories in the

---

[17] Smith xxxii and 6 and 10 (Catherine to Potemkin 21/02/1774).

[18] See Wortman 7: *The literary and dramatic presentations of the monarch where mythic in two senses of the word: they imitated or made reference to heroic and legendary archetypes, and they provided an animating political myth of rule.*

south, accompanied by foreign emissaries, and met with neighbors such as the future Austrian Emperor Joseph II.

During those voyages, which served both as road shows and as inspection tours, the czarina carefully interviewed high- and low-ranking people alike.

(In addition,) I travel not to see places, but people, I know enough about the places through maps, descriptions and information which I could not absorb from a quick visit. What I need is to give people the means to approach me, to allow access to their complaints, and to make those who might abuse my authority fear that I will discover their mistakes, their negligence or the injustices.[19]

In another grand gesture of communication, when Sweden launched a surprise attack on Russia's northern borders in 1788, Catherine immediately went to St. Petersburg, near the front, to lift the people's spirits.[20]

Catherine's prolific writing also built and maintained her reputation. She was well aware that her correspondence, sent by courier across borders, would be intercepted and read. Through her exchange of letters with key French philosophers of the Enlightenment, she gained a reputation as an intellectual, progressive monarch. She was a voracious art collector and assembled a magnificent collection of western masters in the Hermitage. All of this enhanced the image of Russia as modern and westernized.

On the day of her coup, Catherine donned the uniform of Colonel of the Preobrazhensky Guards and rode proudly, saber in hand, at the head of her troops—a scene later immortalized in a portrait (Fig. 5.1). Several important aristocrats, including Princess Dashkova, also in a uniform, accompanied her. This display of leadership linked her with Peter the Great, who had enjoyed the same rank. To commemorate her victories she held public celebrations and erected monuments.

Other than speeches, which she did not favor, Catherine availed herself of the full suite of communication vehicles: theater, portraits, drawings, statues, monuments, coins, dishware, many kinds of writing, and staged public appearances. Her comprehensive communications strategy solidified her power, her impressive achievements, and her legacy.

5.3.8 Generating Positive Change

The territorial, economic, organizational, and modernizing changes that Catherine realized for Russia were as tremendous as they were lasting. A few smaller-scale— but equally positive—reforms are worth noting.

As part of her larger healthcare initiative, Catherine organized a nationwide effort to vaccinate the population against smallpox. She imported the new, somewhat experimental vaccine and invited the doctor who invented it to Russia.

---

[19] Rounding 429.

[20] Smith 251 (Catherine to Potemkin 26/06/1788) and 254 (Catherine to Potemkin 17/07/1788).

Courageously, she had it first administered to herself and to her son Paul. Catherine appeared in public with her son afterward and commemorated the healthcare milestone with a medal in 1772. Also in her education effort, she personally engaged in creating change: she mentored several favorite women pupils at the Smolny Institute.

Catherine's enthusiasm for the ideas of the Enlightenment led her to change practices in criminal law. She abhorred torture and managed to abolish its use in all but name. For example, when Pugachev, who had seriously threatened her power was condemned to a painful death, Catherine secretly intervened to have him killed on the spot, so that he would not suffer.

Some of Catherine's plans to modernize Russia, however, were not realized. She spent much of her formative years at the Russian court immersed in books, in correspondence with philosophers, and in conversation with courtiers and diplomats. Only after taking power did she venture outside, where practical and political realities forced her to backpedal on some of her ideas. As mentioned earlier, she abandoned her wish to abolish serfdom because she needed the support of the Russian nobles.

Catherine adopted a policy of tolerance toward the cultures in the territories she had acquired, as well as their religions (e.g., Islam in the former Turkish lands and Catholicism in the Polish regions), with the exception of the Jews, who had to pay double taxes.

Catherine broke with the Russian tradition of bringing about change by force; instead she used persuasion and education. Key to her success was the decision to immerse herself in Russian culture, language, religion, and rituals and to show respect for traditions before changing them.

In foreign policy, she preferred alliances and deals over battles. Yet, those who dared to stand in her way, such as Pugachev, faced her wrath. She also showed no mercy with the Poles, whose resistance to annexation Catherine violently crushed. Such actions contradicted her Enlightenment values.

5.4 Catherine's Leadership Impact

Two centuries after the Middle Ages ended in Western Europe, Peter the Great took Russia into the modern era. Yet, Russia was still behind. During Catherine's lifetime, Britain started the Industrial Revolution, democracy came to America, and France toppled its king and aristocracy. Russia, ruled by aristocratic landowners, depended on the export of raw materials, and much of its population was enslaved. Nevertheless, Catherine managed to transform Russia into a great power that would forever be involved in Europe's major decisions and conflicts, laying the foundation for its superpower status in the twentieth century. Potemkin, in one of his last letters in 1791 near the end of Catherine's reign, describes Catherine's achievement of growth and modernization well:

(. . .) the most expansive of maps. (. . .) expanded borders, armies, fleets and cities that have multiplied, a populated steppe, peoples who have abandoned savagery, rivers filled with vessels. (and) no longer springs flowing with the blood of the guilty.[21]

It should not come as a surprise then that Catherine has been surnamed The Great.

5.5   What Women Can Learn from This Leader

The accomplishments of Catherine, discussed above, inform this two-part appraisal of her performance:

Leadership Challenge	Rating
Career Direction	*Fully Achieved*
Vision and Strategy for Growth	*Fully Achieved*
Leading a Restructuring Effort	*Fully Achieved*
Renewing Organizational Culture	*Partially Achieved*
Succession Management	*Partially Achieved*

Leadership Competency	Rating
Vision and Strategy Development	*Strong*
Building and Maintaining a Network	*Strong*
Talent Management	*Strong*
Performance Management	*Strong*
Delegation	*Needs Development*
Leveraging Difference	*Strong*
Communication	*Strong*
Generating Positive Change	*Competent*

Catherine II of Russia was highly capable and not afraid of risk. She audaciously seized power with a fairly small power base, which could have backfired if her husband had decided to resist. She chose to lead by the force of her intelligence and knowledge. She saw her role as defending and expanding Russia's borders while raising the Russian population's living standards and level of civilization.

Highly talented herself, Catherine was not jealous of others' gifts. She surrounded herself with talented people, whose performance she managed well. At the same time she was highly controlling and prone to micromanagement. She

---

[21] Smith 382 (Potemkin to Catherine 29/04/1791).

fell into the trap of working extremely hard to do everything herself rather than delegating effectively, thereby leaving Russia without a leadership structure and culture to extend her legacy of reform. When people with fewer talents and less discipline than Catherine came to power, Russia stagnated.

Catherine gathered data and other information effectively and communicated masterfully to a wide audience. She was an expert leader of change, thanks to her communication skills, her evolutionary approach, and her ability to lead by example. Whereas she abhorred cruelty, she did not shrink from using violence against people who stood in her way.

Working effectively with three important lovers, Catherine demonstrated the power of extending professional relationships into the personal realm. Her example also shows that it pays to pick a life partner well: Potemkin shared Catherine's life project, both personally and especially professionally.

As inspiration to modern women leaders, Catherine had three competencies that stand out as her core strengths. First, by developing and implementing a masterful strategy, she advanced Peter the Great's vision of a vast and modern Russia. Second, she prepared herself for the top job by building internal and external networks of people from whom she could learn and extract information—and whom she could later employ to influence key stakeholders. Third, Catherine effectively leveraged her gender by subsuming several positive female archetypes under her unique leadership style. Thus, and through her networking, she was able to neutralize the negative stereotypes of a woman leader, even while maintaining an unconventional lifestyle.

5.6   Top Five Do's and Don'ts from Catherine the Great

- Do
    - Prepare yourself well to take the top job, including by building a network.
    - Nurture close relationships with competent people at work.
    - Reward people for performance.
    - Consider all repercussions while implementing a strategy.
    - Leverage your difference as woman.
- Don't
    - Be a perfectionist. Delegate!
    - Be afraid to rub people the wrong way to defend your principles.
    - Be too tough on people who resist you.
    - Forget to develop a succession plan.
    - Assume that people will immediately understand your logic and intentions.

Bibliography

Carrère d'Encausse, H. (2010). *Catherine II. Un âge d'or pour la Russie*. Paris: Pluriel.

Dixon, S. (2001). *Catherine the great. Profiles in power*. Harlow: Pearson Longman.

Dixon, S. (2009). *Catherine the great*. London: Profile Books.

Fraser, A. (2002). *The warrior queens. Boadiccea's Chariot*. London: Phoenix Press.

Gottschalk, M. (2008). *Königinnen. Fünf Herrscherinnen und ihre Lebensgeschichten*. Weinheim: Beltz & Gelberg.

Neumann-Hoditz, R. (1988). *Katharina II. Die Große*. Reinbek bei Hamburg: Rohwolt Taschenbuch Verlag.

Palmer, R. R. (1964). *The age of the democratic revolution. A political history of Europe and America, 1760–1800. Volume II: The struggle*. Princeton: Princeton University Press.

Rounding, V. (2006). *Catherine the great. Love, sex, and power*. New York: St. Martin's Griffin.

Smith, D. (Ed.). (2005). *Love and conquest: Personal correspondence of Catherine the great and prince Grigory Potemkin*. DeKalb: Northern Illinois University Press.

Winik, J. (2007). *The great upheaval. America and the birth of the modern world, 1788–1800*. New York: HarperCollins.

Wortman, R. S. (1995). *Scenarios of power: Myth and ceremony in Russian monarchy. Volume one: From peter the great to the death of Nicolas I*. Princeton: Princeton University Press.

Four Queens: Lessons in Career Development

6

Drawing parallels between the careers of the four queens and those of modern women might seem like a fool's endeavor. After all, these women achieved their successes in contexts that bear little resemblance to those of today. Indeed, as an executive coach and an expert in leadership development, I fully appreciate the importance of each individual and her unique circumstances when I give career advice. No leader is a clone of her contemporaries, much less of monarchs who lived hundreds of years ago. But leaders often draw wisdom and inspiration from their predecessors, so it is also a fool's endeavor to ignore history, whether recent or remote. In this chapter, I articulate career development lessons from the queens in just that spirit—as women to view as predecessors, as mentors from history.

6.1 Career Development: Getting to the Top and Staying There

6.1.1 Take Practical Steps to Prepare Yourself

Both Elizabeth I and Catherine the Great did not have obvious career paths at first. It was only when rising to the top became a realistic possibility that these two women began to prepare themselves for the eventuality. They lost no time in taking practical steps to get there and developed a clear leadership vision and a strategy. Consequently, both hit the ground running once in power.

Advance preparation has always been one of the best ways to increase the likelihood of eventual success as a leader. Education and on-the-job training are mainstays of preparation for senior roles. No less important is getting in touch with your own values and determining what type of leader you want to be, just as Elizabeth and Catherine did.

P. Vanderbroeck, *Leadership Strategies for Women*, Management for Professionals,
DOI 10.1007/978-3-642-39623-6_6, © Springer-Verlag Berlin Heidelberg 2014

6.1.2 Fend Off the Competition

For the queens, getting to the top and staying there meant dealing with competitors, rebellions, and pretenders to the throne. Staying on top was most difficult for Cleopatra, as she was the only one of the four queens who actually lost the top job to a competitor. She got her job back by leveraging her difference as a woman, and then she dealt ruthlessly with the competition from her siblings.

Without question, making sure that career decision makers are aware of your achievements is helpful. This is quite something else than "selling" yourself and constantly knocking on doors for your next promotion, something women leaders anyway find difficult to do. Yet informing senior management objectively and proactively about positive results and who achieved them is part of your leadership responsibility. Only when all facts are available can the right decisions be taken, including choosing the right person for the job.

In addition, modern women leaders need to identify and suss out direct competitors, as well as others, who may wish to undermine their plans. After all, career competition is an organizational reality. Facing that reality may mean preventing someone else from getting an assignment of strategic importance or high visibility. It also means not backing down in the face of conflict, particularly with competitors. Modern women leaders are often advised to do self-promotion, but disarming competitors is less openly discussed, even though it is an essential element of achieving success.

All of these actions should, of course, remain within ethical boundaries and should add value to the organization. It's best to observe those maxims not merely as a matter of principle but also because it improves your chance of reaching your goals.

6.1.3 Establish Your Legitimacy

Cleopatra's nomination by her father, the previous king, was never contested legally. However, she had to prove her worth in the face of competition. Both her practical achievements and her decision to embrace local Egyptian culture ultimately legitimized her as a leader. Catherine, initially the least "legitimate" of all the queens, proved her unique worth with a burst of legal activity after overthrowing the government. The key lesson is to set yourself apart from the competition.

The queens had to meet the double challenge of proving that a woman could serve effectively in the top job and that they, as individuals, deserved it. All four queens achieved quick wins early in their tenure, which allowed them to establish credibility outside the military domain for which they lacked training. They also successfully leveraged their femininity by drawing parallels with positive female archetypes, most often that of protective and caring mother.

Proving that you deserve to be in a leadership role remains a challenge for women in modern organizations, particularly at the highest levels. Leadership is still more often associated with men than with women. A focus on getting visible results soon after entering a new role is therefore fundamental. The lesson provided by history is: First build your credibility by seizing opportunities in areas of strength; then expand your influence to other areas by surrounding yourself with competent people who can compensate for your limitations. This is more effective than attempting to master all domains yourself.

Besides needing to prove that a woman deserves the role, a woman leader often finds herself having to *disprove* that she is in the role as a "token" or "quota" woman. The key, as the queens demonstrate, is to turn difference into opportunity. (See Chap. 7 for more on how to leverage difference.)

6.1.4   Identify Mentors

Cleopatra's career success was bolstered by the mentoring she received from two experienced leaders: her father and Julius Caesar. Isabella of Spain carefully chose personal confessors who served as coaches and mentors. Elizabeth, even before becoming queen, benefited from the mentorship of William Cecil, 13 years her senior, whom she eventually appointed as her First Secretary. Being mentored throughout one's career will always be important. Just as the queens were not too proud to seek guidance from talented people, any leader today should confidently embrace mentors who offer essential opportunities for learning.

A salient point is that all four queens benefited from senior mentors: individuals more mature and experienced than themselves. Modern women leaders should seek out such individuals within their own organization and beyond. It should be individuals who can help resolving leadership dilemmas, offer advice with identifying career options, can open doors to their network, provide sponsorship, and help navigate the organizational culture. Given the still existing gender imbalance at senior levels, more often than not such mentors will be men. The resulting diversity in the mentor-mentee relationship may well produce additional synergies.

6.1.5   Build Strong Relationships

The queens cultivated two types of emotional relationships that enhanced their careers.

Personal Relationships at Work

Crossing the boundary between the professional and the personal was typical of all four queens, and choosing the right partners became an important factor in their leadership success. Having someone to spar with and confide in made the queens feel less lonely at the top. Such relationships also compensated for professional deficits, notably in military affairs.

Isabella and Ferdinand became a true husband-and-wife team, both at work and at home. Catherine combined love and work successfully and sequentially with three men. After an intense and fairly short love affair with Potemkin, she maintained a highly successful professional and emotional friendship with him as her second in command.

Women, more than men, form emotional connections with their colleagues. That can sometimes create difficulty if, for example, they take negative feedback as evidence of a break in the emotional bond or find themselves in the position of needing to fire someone with whom they feel connected. Rather than to avoid these challenges, the lesson of the queens is to have relationships that are both objective *and* subjective. Yes, that might mean taking your personal feelings into account when selecting a team member (though, of course, without making it the only consideration). It is practical for women leaders to develop relationships, with both male and female colleagues that have a personal dimension. Not only does it give you greater access to wisdom from those people, but it also reduces loneliness.

Unfortunately, the importance of close personal relationships at work gets lost in many modern organizations. Work can often be characterized by short-lived professional connections; an emphasis on purely objective, data-based decision making; uniformity of dress and lack of self-expression; and fear of sexual harassment claims. Each of these elements has their appropriate place in workplace policies, but if they are overapplied, they can undermine people's capacity to form strong bonds.

Many women have been socialized to share questions and problems openly with sisters, mothers, and female friends, so they may find it easier to do the same in a trusting relationship at work. Women leaders often have this advantage over their male counterparts. The key seems to be in choosing the competent person, as three of the four queens did effectively. And, of course, befriending incompetent people can become a liability, as for Elizabeth I. You also must avoid allowing your positive feelings toward someone to excuse poor performance from that person.

Life Partners

Except for Elizabeth, the queens choose one or more life partners who shared both their personal and professional aspirations. Together they achieved more than they would have alone. Catherine the Great learned this the hard way, through a failed marriage. After that, she had a string of professionally useful love affairs. Isabella stands out as the queen who, rather than depending on a chance encounter, single-mindedly targeted a specific individual—Ferdinand—with whom she managed to have a romantic, loving, stable relationship.

Of course, ideas about love and marriage have evolved greatly over the centuries. The bottom line is simply to make your personal and professional lives mutually reinforcing. Obviously, you and your life partner need not work for the same organization. Whereas love is the basis of a good marriage, falling in love with a partner who shares your mission in both your work *and* your life strengthens the foundation of a leadership career. Openly discussing and negotiating a win-win deal may well be part of this: For instance, Isabella and Ferdinand agreed first to realize her career goal (Spain's reunification) and then his (Aragon's expansion in the Mediterranean).

6.1.6 Make Work/Life Balance a Priority

All four queens had the advantage of plenty of staff around them to help with domestic duties. Still, Cleopatra and Isabella took the time to look after their children, as both had husbands whose career obligations often kept them away from home. Yet, the queens took care of themselves and found opportunities to relax from the burdens of work. They loved outdoor sports such as horse riding and hunting. Cleopatra indulged in boozy nights of laughter with Antony. Isabella took pleasure in good meals, accompanied by the music of the court musicians. Elizabeth loved to throw parties and dance. Catherine enjoyed reading, writing, and intellectual debates.

The queens' approach to work/life balance confirms what nowadays is generally recognized as essential: an infrastructure that allows women leaders to integrate work and family. It should be high on the priority list when negotiating the terms and conditions of a new job or promotion.

6.2 How Can Organizations Help Women Have Successful Leadership Careers?

The following four recommendations do not represent a comprehensive program for career development. They are simply the most salient lessons that organizations can take from the lives of the accomplished queens.

6.2.1 Leadership Development

Women deserve leadership-development initiatives that are tailored to their needs. They may require more help in identifying and landing the right assignments and projects that prepare them specifically for senior roles. Apart from skill building, efforts should offer opportunities to reflect on and discuss values, so that women can discover, develop, and leverage their own unique leadership styles for their career progression.

6.2.2 Build Awareness

Organizations can help their leaders become more attuned to the differences between men and women leaders. This will improve the effectiveness of efforts to find the right person for the right job. Rather than trying to "fix" women to make them "suitable" for leadership positions, organizations should work to create a gender bilingual culture so that perceptions measured by 360° evaluations are not influenced by unconscious biases against women.

6.2.3 Provide Mentoring Opportunities

Well-designed mentoring programs may give a better return on investment than expensive skills-training programs. A good mentoring program involves identifying, incentivizing, training, evaluating, and connecting mentors. This includes helping both mentors (i.e. senior men) and mentees (i.e. younger women) dealing effectively with being very different from another.

6.2.4 Encourage Work/Life Balance

Organizations need to value an infrastructure that makes it easier to integrate career and family. Both internal initiatives and collaborations with local government and other community organizations can be instrumental in this effort.

In summary, to manage and leverage women's leadership talent effectively, organizations need to recognize that women and men have different leadership development needs, motivational needs, and different career needs. It would be wise for organizations to open up their leadership development process, compensation and benefits system, and career tracks to make them more flexible in order to respond to gender differences.

6.3 The Final Question: Did These Queens Actively Promote Gender Diversity?

The little evidence we have seems to indicate that this issue was not on their radars. After all, discussions of equality between men and women in the workplace started some 50 years after Catherine the Great, the last of the four queens, finished her reign.

Cleopatra and Marc Antony treated their daughter the same as their sons: She was named ruler of individual parts of the realm. Isabella of Spain gave her daughters a better and more useful education than she had received. Yet, by favoring her son over his older sister as future king, she emphasized the realization of her vision (Spain's unification) over eliminating the negative bias toward female offspring in the succession laws of Castile, Isabella's homeland. Her husband and co-ruler Ferdinand, on the contrary, went much further: He picked a fight with the parliament of his home country, Aragon, much more powerful than Castile's parliament, to abolish the ancient law that kept his daughter from succeeding him. Having had the experience of working closely with a competent woman, Ferdinand had come a long way since his early days, when he had become very upset at being called Isabella's husband rather than king.

Elizabeth I and Catherine the Great had women as their immediate predecessors. Given their track record, both Mary Tudor and Tsarina Elisabeth seemed to confirm the bias that women were unsuited to rule. Both Elizabeth I and Catherine proved that stereotype wrong. Elizabeth, however, did nothing to further the cause of women, as she may not have seen the need. As a matter of fact, her closest competitor for the top job was a woman: Mary Queen of Scots. Catherine also had a contemporary female counterpart: Maria Theresia, the devout Empress of Austria. Catherine invested in the education of women and men alike as part of her long-term strategy to fill Russia's talent pipeline. Although she personally mentored some of the pupils, the main objective of Catherine's Smolny Institute for noble women was to help women become better at their traditional roles of mother and educator.

The queens kept within the traditional boundaries of their eras. And although they had to push many a boundary to be successful, the gender divide was not one of them. In fact, in some cases, men around them were more willing to push such boundaries.

Bibliography

Clutterbuck, D., Poulsen, K. M., & Kochan, F. (2012). *Developing successful diversity mentoring programmes: An international case book*. Maidenhead: Open University Press.

Eagly, A. H., & Carli, L. L. (2007). *Through the Labyrinth: The truth about how women become leaders*. Boston: Harvard Business School Press.

Ibarra, H. (1992). Homophily and differential returns: Sex differences in network structure and access in an advertising firm. *Administrative Science Quarterly, 37*, 422–447.

de Janasz, S. C., Sullivan, S. E., & Whiting, V. (2003). Mentor networks and career success: Lessons for turbulent times. *The Academy of Management Executive, 17*(4), 78–91.

Kremen Bolton, M. (2000). *The third shift: Managing hard choices in our careers, homes, and lives as women*. New York: Jossey-Bass.

Vanderbroeck, P. (2010). The traps that keep women from reaching the top and how to avoid them. *The Journal of Management Development, 29*(9), 764–770.

Wittenberg-Cox, A. (2010). *How women mean business: A step by step guide to profiting from gender balanced business*. Chichester: Wiley.

This chapter, like Chap. 6, aims to show how our four queens can serve as mentors from history for today's women leaders. Specifically, let's turn our attention to the nine leadership competencies about which we have the most historical evidence and, also, the most practical lessons. In short, these nine dimensions of leadership are what made the queens successful and, occasionally, led them to fail.

7.1 Leadership Competencies: Strengths and Weaknesses

The table below compares the four queens using the competency ratings that were listed for them individually at the end of Chaps. 2, 3, 4 and 5. Green means rated as *strong,* blue as *competent*, and red as *needs development*. A blank indicates insufficient evidence for an evaluation. The competency in which the queens, as a group, performed best is listed at the top, followed by the remaining eight in descending order of their collective performance.

P. Vanderbroeck, *Leadership Strategies for Women*, Management for Professionals, DOI 10.1007/978-3-642-39623-6_7, © Springer-Verlag Berlin Heidelberg 2014

Leadership Competency	Cleopatra	Isabella	Elizabeth	Catherine
Leveraging Difference	Strong	Strong	Strong	Strong
Communication		Strong	Strong	Strong
Talent Management		Strong	Competent	Strong
Vision & Strategy Development	Competent	Strong	Needs Development	Strong
Generating Positive Change	Strong	Competent		Competent
Giving & Receiving Feedback		Competent	Strong	
Performance Management			Needs Development	Strong
Building & Maintaining a Network	Needs Development			Strong
Team Leadership & Delegation			Competent	Needs Development

Modern leadership frameworks include most of the nine competencies listed above, with the exception of leveraging one's difference as a woman. That's because existing frameworks generally are based on how men succeed within male-dominated organizations.

Leveraging difference is the one competency that was an essential ingredient of success for all four queens, even though alone it would not have been enough. None of these four women would have achieved as much without leveraging her difference in a male environment. All four reached the top and stayed there for a long time because they were able to overcome biases against women and turn difference into opportunity.

Nevertheless, leveraging difference is not the only competency for which women leaders, including our queens, tend to have a natural affinity; communication and talent management are two others. However, evidence does show that women leaders are more likely than their male counterparts to underestimate the importance of networking and the need to delegate.

7.2 Leadership Lessons

Nine leadership lessons emerge from the competencies that the four queens used to meet their leadership challenges. The lessons, articulated in the pages that follow, are intended merely to be sources of inspiration and insight as you develop your own leadership style—not as a how-to list or a one-size-fits-all prescription.

7.2.1 Leverage Your Difference as a Woman in Your Professional Context

Early in her career, Cleopatra showed that not leveraging your difference as a woman (i.e., by imitating men) can cost you the top job. Isabella, by identifying with positive female archetypes, successfully fought against the bias of being considered second best simply because she was a woman. At the same time, she managed her reputation well by observing what was expected of her in the roles of queen, wife, and mother.

All four queens publicly identified themselves with positive female archetypes: the fair queen or damsel in distress who seeks help from a noble knight, the seductive woman, the protecting and caring mother, the wise and stern school teacher, the female warrior, the morally pure virgin. This strategy allowed them to capitalize on their uniqueness and authenticity as women while neutralizing the perception that women might not be able to lead effectively. And by switching deftly among archetypes, they avoided the trap of being cast in a single, negative female stereotype.

It should be no surprise that people perceive leaders differently depending on their gender. Psychologists have found that people primarily associate women with being "communal". For example, women are often expected to be affectionate, gentle, sensitive, helpful, and caring. Men, in contrast, elicit "agentic" associations, such as dominance, aggression, ambition, confidence, and individualism. Because leadership is often associated with agentic or male stereotypes, women are often perceived as less suited for leadership.

To be successful, women leaders need to exhibit both communal and agentic qualities. However, doing that with authenticity can be difficult. After all, women who behave in stereotypically male ways are often perceived negatively. That is why following the adage "Do-as-the-boys-do" can prevent women from reaching the top. Women are, in fact, in a double bind. If they are seen as too agentic, they risk having an air of inauthenticity; if they are too communal, they may be perceived as less suited for leadership.

The solution for women leaders is not to fight stereotypes but to leverage them. The lesson from history lies in the identifying with positive female archetypes. All four queens succeeded in untying the double bind by making clear that their agentic qualities were derived from archetypical female models, not by imitating men.

Female archetypes are still alive in our society, but with different identifiers than what the queens had at their disposal. Few modern women would want to identify, for example, with the Virgin Mary. But Pallas Athena still carries a resonant archetype, even though her name is not as familiar as in the days of our queens. In the fictional TV series *Desperate Housewives*, set in an affluent American suburb, the archetypical women involved in the mythological cat fight that set off the Trojan War reappear. The characters are Pallas Athena, the proper teacher-type with the moral high ground (Bree); Aphrodite, the beautiful seductress (Gabriella); Hera, the caring mother who can be aggressive when her family is threatened (Lynette); Helen, the fair maiden in need of rescue (Susan); and Eris, the goddess of discord keen on crashing the party (Eadie). These characters annoy the audience because they are stereotypical, yet they also amuse viewers because their monotypical roles still resonate as believable archetypes.

Modern women leaders do not need to take on masculine characteristics to be agentic. The teacher and the mother for example are positive female archetypes representing legitimate authority and power. Was not Margaret Thatcher's influence based on her posing as the unflinching stern teacher of the nation? I have personally watched female executive coaches exercise remarkable authority over groups of A-type executives by embodying the stern teacher.

Sometimes it even helps to explicitly reference such archetypes. Rear Admiral Margaret Klein, who broke through the glass ceiling in the U.S. Navy, told her male subordinates, "Think of me as your mother in uniform." The bottom line is that a woman leader who assumes a male, agentic posture is *not* perceived as being authentic, even if it reflects her true character. However, exhibiting agentic behavior associated with a female archetype *is* perceived as authentic.

Using positive female archetypes can help to reinforce communal attributes, too. Margaret Thatcher again provides an example. During the Falklands War in the 1980s, she penned personal letters to the families of soldiers killed in action. She wrote that, as the first British prime minister who was also a mother of a son, she could fully empathize with their loss. That masterful leveraging of difference as a woman while referring to a positive female archetype (an authentic gesture for Thatcher, by all accounts) is a tough act for any man to follow. The Falklands War was controversial from the start, and it became even more so as soldiers got killed. Thatcher's behavior was a key factor in maintaining British citizens' support for her strategy.

Recent studies have shown that archetypical female qualities such as charm can be used effectively in the workplace. Former U.S. Secretary of State Madeleine Albright, for example, admitted to using her feminine charm in bilateral negotiations with foreign dignitaries.

Both the queens and modern women leaders have used archetypical female leadership roles to show that they can lead effectively while remaining authentic. Identification with or being inspired by particular archetypes helps to expand a woman leader's behavioral repertoire. What is more, when women feel they are being stereotyped in an unflattering way, it can negatively affect their performance—what psychologists call "stereotype threat".[1] Using a recognizable positive image—an archetype of your choice—as an antidote to a stereotype can be very useful. Such leveraging of difference is more effective than fighting cultural perceptions tooth-and-nail.

Does embodying an archetype mean dressing up like Pallas Athena in the office? Of course not. To get the results you want, simply be authentic. First be yourself (a woman) rather than someone you are not (a man). Second, perform the on-stage drama of leadership so that it resonates positively with the subconscious perceptions of the people you lead. Don't hesitate to identify for yourself the characters, images, and stories that reflect positive female archetypes for the nation, culture, and organization you inhabit. Archetypes are locked into our collective unconscious and therefore timeless. Over the centuries they have continuously inspired new ideas and interpretations. Positive archetypes thus can become allies of the modern woman leader by adapting them to the modern context. And, third, don't forget: While leveraging your difference as a woman, draw (as the queens did) on multiple archetypes, to avoid being locked into a single stereotype. In short, be a multitypical—not a monotypical—woman leader.[2]

7.2.2 Communication: Be Present and Visible

The queens were strong communicators who usually exploited a large suite of communication vehicles to convey messages and build their images and reputations. These included staged public appearances, road shows, theater, slogans, visual imagery and symbols, verbal and written communication. All four were power dressers who wanted to be seen, not to fade into the background. Yet each had her strengths. Isabella was quick to adopt the new communication technology of the printing press. Catherine was particularly competent in all forms of written communication. Elizabeth I, the strongest communicator of the four, was unmatched in public speaking.

Clearly, all leaders, women and men alike, benefit from using a wide portfolio of communication tools. In addition, women leaders should leverage the fact that they stand out as exceptions in contexts where men are in the majority. They can use that

---

[1] For example stereotypes like: "A woman leader cannot be tough." "Executives don't take lessons from female business school professors."

[2] For example, if you choose to use your feminine charm to open a door at work, you may want to appear as the proper teacher or the mother on the next occasion, lest you get locked into a stereotype. In any case, do take a moment after the event to evaluate your impact.

reality to get attention and be heard, though skillfully of course. In a situation where you want to exercise power, dress and act the part; in a context where you want to ask for support, present yourself in a way that fits that venue. And when you find yourself alone in an all-male environment, why not address the elephant in the room explicitly, as Elizabeth did?

7.2.3 Select and Develop Talented People

Isabella introduced a meritocratic staffing process, built up a pool of high-potentials, and invested in training and developing them. She had a penchant for technological innovation and for choosing innovative people for key positions. Catherine had both a short- and a long-term perspective on talent management. She was good at selecting talented direct reports, and she actively assigned and reassigned them according to their abilities and performance. For the long term, Catherine invested in training and education to create a talent pipeline to meet Russia's future management needs.

It's no surprise that effective talent management helps a leader and is increasingly important in modern organizations. What may not be obvious is that talent management is one competency for which women seem to have a special aptitude. To capitalize on this aptitude women leaders can take personal responsibility for coaching and mentoring talented individuals. At a more senior level, they can create systems and processes to ensure that people development happens permanently throughout their organization. The overall impact should be an increase in productivity, as long as it is combined with delegation (see Sect. 7.2.9 below).

7.2.4 Develop an Inspiring Vision to Reach Your Strategic Goals

With the exception of Elizabeth, all of the queens were not only good at developing a vision and a strategy, but also at implementing them. Conventional wisdom holds that vision is an area of weakness for women leaders, but that perception has been shown to originate with male-biased filters that don't adequately reflect reality. The three visionary queens also took the risks necessary to implement their strategies.

Cleopatra developed two visions sequentially. She put in place an effective strategy to realize the first: to become a strategic supplier to Rome. And she got quite far in realizing the second: independence from Rome. Isabella, in contrast, fully developed and realized two sequential visions: unification and overseas expansion (using a strategy of reconquest, restructuring and renewal). Giving the go-ahead to Columbus, in particular, was a daring exploit. Catherine's vision of a modernized and strong Russia was realized through a strategy of education, legislation, and bold military campaigns. She also used sound data analysis to make decisions, managed resources effectively, and made strategically savvy deals with potential competitors.

The message from history is that women leaders can develop a vision that inspires followers to high performance so that strategic goals are achieved. The queens had the courage to take the risks necessary to yield high returns.

7.2.5 Leverage Difference to Generate Positive Change

Interestingly, all four queens inherited a messy combination of financial debt and political instability. It is difficult to say whether they simply drew the short straw among their male counterparts. What is certain, however, is that they made cleaning up the mess a priority, giving them an opportunity to prove themselves. For example, they implemented innovative solutions to financial problems, such as unprecedented monetary reforms. Being a woman actually made it easier for them to bring about unconventional change. If they had not crossed some ethical boundaries, this leadership competency would have ranked, collectively, as one of their top strengths.

Cleopatra, in a difficult co-ruler position confronting both Rome's power and Egypt's dire straits, effectively pushed boundaries to place herself at the top of the organization. She also cultivated succession candidates in Egypt who had a strong connection with Rome, and she transformed a loss-making organization into a profitable one.

Isabella became an effective agent of change by simultaneously addressing culture and structure: She combined a common value system plus a joint purpose with a unified leadership and a reinforced organizational structure. Yet her record is tainted by her employment of ruthless and useless methods—namely, the Inquisition and the expulsion of Jews and Muslims.

Being handed a mess is an opportunity to prove that you can clean it up, and in many environments a woman leader is more easily accepted as an agent of change—from a person who is different, different things are expected. Start by going for quick wins in the areas where you are strong. Then find talented people to compensate for your weaknesses.

7.2.6 Give Effective Feedback to Increase the Organization's Productivity

Of the four queens, Elizabeth ranks strongest in this competency. Not only did she give effective, fact-based feedback. She also clearly mentioned the positive or negative impact of the behavior she had observed, including the emotional impact. In addition, she identified for the recipient of the feedback which impacts were most important to address in making improvements. She was also aware of the emotional impact her feedback could have and used the feedback to reset expectations. At the same time she was open to constructive feedback from her staff and encouraged them to speak up. Elizabeth did sometimes make it abundantly clear that she did not like the feedback she received, but she listened nonetheless (even, for example, to advice that marrying Leicester was not a good idea). However, Elizabeth also proved that effective performance management takes more than just delivering good feedback.

Feedback in all directions—upward, sideways, downward—helps the people who are close to a leader improve. But the feedback must be clear, respectful, and fact-based. And it must be given with a keen awareness of how it may be received, including at an emotional level. Not everybody takes negative feedback, even if it is objective, in stride. This may be the case especially for people with whom the leader has a close personal relationship.

7.2.7   Manage Your Team to High Performance

Catherine the Great effectively motivated her managers by combining an inspiring vision with real opportunities for financial gain, as did Isabella. Catherine was best in class when it came to performance management. Like Elizabeth, she was willing to give people a second chance, but she knew when to stop being supportive and replace someone who was failing. She tolerated serious mistakes only from people with a strong track record. She even took this competency to a strategic level by introducing an organization-wide performance-appraisal system.

The key takeaway message is to adeptly mix objective and subjective assessments of people. Know your own limit for tolerating colleagues whom you like but who may not meet your performance expectations. Other than that, adhere to usual good practices for performance management: Find out what really motivates your followers, and use your inspiring vision to hit their motivational buttons, which may differ from your own.

7.2.8   Build and Maintain a Network, Particularly to Manage Your Reputation

Lack of networking skills became a career killer for Cleopatra. She failed to recognize the importance of informal networks behind the formal hierarchy. She also did not appreciate how networking can positively influence a reputation. In her dealings with key stakeholders, she favored the "what" over the "how". As a result, she was on her own when she really needed people to vouch for her.

Catherine, again, was greatest in this competency. The network she built was vital to reaching the top and staying there. Throughout her career she deliberately built and maintained good personal relationships with a large number of people, both inside and outside Russia. Those contacts gave her useful input that helped her to resolve issues with European competitors without the need for head-on conflict.

Beyond the traditional function of networking (to access strategic information and build a group of supporters), using a network to build and protect a positive reputation is particularly important for women, as they seek to show that they can perform as well as men. Absent a network, Cleopatra's reputation among the Romans was being sullied without her knowing it or being able to do something about it. Catherine, whose lifestyle posed a major risk to her reputation, did use networking to counteract negative biases. She was a credible leader from day one in the job.

Networking helps any leader, but for women it also aids in managing potentially negative misperceptions related to gender. People interpret who you are and what you do through their own cultural, organizational, psychological, and other filters. Bad reputations can be built purely on the fact that, as a woman, you are different from leaders who may have come before. So it is important to proactively influence how people see you by skillfully cultivating useful connections.

7.2.9   Delegate to Competent People

Catherine, as a perfectionist and an extremely hard worker, did a lot on her own. Very few people could meet her high standards. She was willing to share authority with a person whose qualities she truly admired, but apart from Potemkin, no one really made the grade. By working one-on-one with her direct reports, she failed to create a viable team around herself.

Isabella created an effective management team, the *Consejo Real*. Her delegating certain leadership tasks to Ferdinand according to his strengths illustrates that Isabella was willing to share authority. Still, she kept tabs on what was happening on the battlefield, and she sometimes intervened when objectives where not met.

Getting others to work for you is key to maximizing your output as a leader. Assigning roles, responsibilities, and tasks to subordinates and letting them get on with it is an area where men typically have an edge. Women leaders often need to fully trust someone before they will delegate. A woman may therefore find it most appealing to use her strength in selecting and developing talented people in order to find those who are truly trustworthy and, therefore, worthy of delegation.

7.3   How Can Organizations Fully Develop Women Leaders?

7.3.1   Let Women Be Women

The most important lesson is to get women out of the "Men-and-women-are-alike" trap. Measuring women's behavior according to pretentiously gender-neutral, but actually male standards (i.e. based on what makes men successful leaders in male-dominated organizations) does both women and the organizations that wish to cultivate their talents a disfavor. It forces women into a behavioral framework that is more suited to men than to women. Organizations therefore need to review and update their talent-management processes and systems (e.g. competency frameworks and 360° evaluations) to ensure they are gender bilingual and remove hidden biases against women.

7.3.2 Tailor Leadership Development According to Gender

When companies have accepted that women and men are not 100 % alike in their leadership, it makes sense to dedicate part of the leadership-development effort to women's specific needs. History has confirmed that, on balance, women find delegation more challenging than men do. So it makes sense to give extra attention to this competency in developing women leaders. The same goes for helping women turn strong relationships at work into an asset rather than a liability as they manage subordinates' performance.

7.3.3 Help Women Network

Organizations should provide opportunities for women to network across the organization and with key stakeholders such as external clients. This adds more value than maintaining an internal women's network. Managers and mentors should allow and encourage their talented female staff to network, not least to build and maintain a positive reputation.

What leaders do not always realize, however, is that different networks have different uses. To get useful and honest advice you may want to network outside your usual personal and professional networks, so that you connect with people who are not in some way dependent on you or in competition with you. A practical way to do this is by attending events, where you will meet peers from different industries, countries and backgrounds.

In summary, to maximize the potential of women leaders organizations need to admit that—surprise, surprise—women in certain respects are different from men. Organizations can use such differences to their advantage by ensuring that behavior by women leaders is perceived in its true light and appreciated for its true value. Organizations that want to maximize the opportunity of gender diversity at the top need to differentiate their leadership development according to gender—if they are to benefit from a gender-balanced, and therefore high-performing, leadership team.

Bibliography

Babcock, L., & Laschever, S. (2003). *Women don't ask: Negotiation and the gender divide*. Princeton, NJ: Princeton University Press.

Baxter, J. (2012). Women of the corporation: A sociolinguistic perspective of senior women's leadership language in the UK. *Journal of Sociolinguistics, 16*(1), 81–107.

Beard, A. (2009). Hot or not. Attractive people are more successful at work. Should we do anything about it? *Harvard Business Review, October*, 144–145.

Carli, L. L., & Eagly, A. H. (2012). Leadership and gender. In D. V. Day & J. Antonakis (Eds.), *The nature of leadership* (2nd ed., pp. 437–478). Thousand Oaks, CA: Sage.

Eagly, A. H., & Carli, L. L. (2007). *Through the Labyrinth: The truth about how women become leaders*. Boston: Harvard Business School Press.

Kabacoff, R. I. (1998). *Gender differences in organizational leadership: A large sample study. Management research group research paper*. Portland, ME: Management Research Group.

Kabacoff, R., & Peters, H. (1998). *The way women and men lead—Different, but equally effective. Management research group research report*. Portland, ME: Management Research Group.

Kets De Vries, M. F. R., Vrignaudb, P., Agrawalc, A., & Florent-Treacy, E. (2010). Development and application of the leadership archetype questionnaire. *International Journal of Human Resource Management, 21*(15), 2848–2863.

Koenig, A. M., Eagly, A. H., Mitchell, A. A., & Ristikari, T. (2011). Are leader stereotypes masculine? A meta-analysis of three research paradigms. *Psychological Bulletin, 137*(4), 616–642.

Kray, L. J., Locke, C. C., & Van Zant, A. B. (2012). Feminine charm: An experimental analysis of its costs and benefits. *Personality and Social Psychology Bulletin, XX*(X), 1–15.

Olsson, S., & Walker, R. (2003). Through a gendered lens? Male and female executives' representations of one another. *Leadership & Organization Development Journal, 34*(7), 387–396.

Van den Poel, M. (2012). *Delegation as the key enabler for senior female leadership transitions: An exploratory study* (Thesis for the executive masters in coaching and consulting for change). Fontainebleau: INSEAD.

Vanderbroeck, P. (2010a). The traps that keep women from reaching the top and how to avoid them. *The Journal of Management Development, 29*(9), 764–770.

Vanderbroeck, P. (2010b). Lonely leaders: And how organizations can help them. *The International Journal of Mentoring and Coaching, VIII*(1), 83–90.

Wittenberg-Cox, A. (2010). *How women mean business. A step by step guide to profiting from gender balanced business*. Chichester: Wiley.

Index

P. Vanderbroeck, *Leadership Strategies for Women*, Management for Professionals, DOI 10.1007/978-3-642 39623-6, © Springer-Verlag Berlin Heidelberg 2014